Winning
THROUGH
Integrity

Winning
THROUGH
Integrity
Cliff C. Jones

Abingdon Press
Nashville

WINNING THROUGH INTEGRITY

Copyright © 1985 by Abingdon Press

This book is printed on acid-free paper.

Library of Congress Cataloging-in-Publication Data

Jones, Cliff C., 1919-
  Winning through integrity.
  1. Christian life—1960-
BV4501.2.J5858   1985   248.4   85-9177

ISBN 0-687-45604-5 (alk. paper)

Scripture quotations are from the Revised Standard Version of the Bible,
copyrighted 1946, 1952, © 1971, 1973 by the Division of Christian Education of the
National Council of the Churches of Christ in the U.S.A., and are used by
permission. Quotations noted KJV are from the King James Version of the Bible.

Excerpt from "The Rich Man" from *Tobogganing on Parnassus* by Franklin P. Adams.
Copyright © 1911 by Doubleday and Co., Inc. Reprinted by permission of the
publisher.

Manufactured by the Parthenon Press at
Nashville, Tennessee, United States of America

To Patricia,
whose brilliant suggestions materially improved each
chapter of this book, and to Barbara Bartocci, who
continued to insist that I should write it

Contents

Winning
THROUGH
Integrity

Chapter One

WHY THIS BOOK?

Maybe you've read—or at least seen on the bookstore racks—all the "how-to" books designed to help you navigate the rough shoals of business. Authors are quick to tell you how to survive in the executive jungle, how to play organization politics, and how to look out for Number One.

Sage warnings are given about learning the corporate "game," spotting the guy who's out to knife you in the back, stepping over the competition to climb the next rung of success.

"Nice guys finish last" is handed out as a business truism, followed by, "Don't get mad; get even."

It would appear that many Americans have a restlessness of spirit and a disillusionment with their present conditions. There is a longing for something—often summed up by the vaguely understood term *success*.

We do have solid data that millions of Americans are not leading what we consider to be overall successful lives. Here is an abbreviated list of statistics furnished by the Mental Health Association:

Item: Depression affects an estimated thirty million people in the United States.

Item: In one year, doctors write more than sixty million prescriptions for Valium, one for every four Americans.

Item: Those with a mental problem or an emotional illness that impairs functioning number 15 to 25 percent of the population.

Item: One out of ten children is born illegitimate.

Item: Nearly one-half the marriages now end in divorce.

Item: Of industrial accidents, 85 percent are believed to have underlying factors of mental or emotional disturbances.

Why should this be so when corresponding millions of how-to books promising brilliant success and glowing happiness have been purchased?

The Bible consistently remains at the top of the best sellers. People continue to buy it. What we don't know is how many read the Bible with the understanding that it is a manual for successfully dealing with all aspects of life—both its triumphs and its failures.

I do not believe that mankind was engineered for failure any more than a personal computer is engineered to fail. Anyone who has a computer knows two facts. It would be folly to attempt to operate it successfully without first reading the operating instructions. And, even after reading them, it will be necessary to have someone explain many of the hard to understand portions.

That is what this book is intended to do—to explain some of the instructions that a Christian or a Jew reads in his Bible. Instructions that the test of time has proven can make the difference between failure and success in business or in any aspect of life.

Just for fun, let's look at two extremes of personalities you're apt to meet in business. We'll call the first one the Apple type after a hypothetical individual, Mr. or Ms. Apple.

(For sheer ease of language, I shall use "he" to designate the Apple individual and "she" to designate the Berry individual. "He" or "she" could apply to either individual, of course.)

The Apple type is financially insecure. No matter how high his salary bracket, his energies are often drained by money worries. He is chronically anxious and fearful and generally pessimistic. He is also often depressed, unhappy, and he scoffs at the idea of prayer.

The second type we'll call the Berry type after Mr. or Ms. Berry. The Berry type manages her personal finances well so that, no matter what the income level, she avoids really serious money problems. She feels little anxiety and faces the future unafraid. Although she may sometimes feel blue, she is seldom depressed for very long. She is a prayerful person and believes in the power of prayer.

Now, of course, these two types fall at the opposite ends of a spectrum. There are variations in each type all along the line in between.

But, whether you are closer to the Berry or to the Apple depends, I'm convinced, on how you have integrated Judeo-Christian principles into your life.

Or, put it another way: if you practice certain biblical precepts, the odds are in your favor that you will achieve more significant success than the person who ignores what the instruction manual on successful living has to say. Why? Because instruction manuals are designed to keep you from making mistakes. They will, too, provided you read them carefully and can understand them. One of the more difficult parts of any manual may be the unusual words it employs. Before you can really follow its directions, you must find out the special meaning those particular words have. Let's look at one of those special words with a surprising meaning in the next chapter.

Chapter Two

WHAT IS THIS THING CALLED SIN?
The Ten Commandments and Business

In his book *Whatever Became of Sin?* Dr. Karl Menninger gives one definition of the word *sin* as "behavior which pains or harms or destroys my neighbor—or me, myself."

That's a good, concise definition, but let's expand on it a bit. Back in the fourteenth century in England a man named John Wycliffe commenced the first English translation of the Bible. He worked directly from the Bible called the Vulgate, written in Latin. In his work he very quickly came across the Latin word *peccatum*, which meant "error" or "fault." This word appeared so often he also may have checked with the Hebrew language Bible. The word used there was *Ahvoair*, which meant "missing the mark." The sense was that of an archer who aimed his arrow at a target and because he misjudged the distance, he failed to hit the target or mark.

For some reason, old John Wycliffe chose to translate these words as *sin*. Now consider a minute what a difference in our thinking there might be today if Wycliffe six hundred years ago had decided to use the word *mistake* instead of *sin*.

If you read the Bible by substituting *mistake* for wherever it says *sin*, it begins to sound a lot more like an instruction manual.

Similarly, you can give yourself a bit of a shock by referring to an error in today's world as a sin rather than a mistake. For example, suppose you are the CEO (chief executive officer) of a business that is acquiring another firm. You are going to merge that firm into your company. There are tax consequences and many other pitfalls to avoid in such a merger. Of course, you will employ competent legal counsel every step of the way. It would be a *sin* (mistake) not to do so.

Now how does that sound? It's rather like saying that it's a sin to add two and two and get five! So, it may sound weird to use *sin* in this way, but it is not only permissible but highly instructive to substitute *mistake* for *sin* in many of the Bible passages.

Let's look at some easy ones—ten actions that we have all been taught are sins. Most of us can remember only a few of the Ten Commandments. These are the ten sins, or mistakes, that God told Moses to instruct his people to avoid at all cost. These ten are basic and very generalized instructions on what pitfalls to avoid if we desire a successful life. Let's list them for ready reference and then make comments concerning their application to modern business success.

1. You shall have no other gods before me.
2. You shall not worship graven images.
3. You shall not take the name of the Lord, your God, in vain.
4. Remember the sabbath day, to keep it holy. Six days you shall labor, but the seventh day . . . you shall not do any work.
5. Honor your father and your mother, that your days may be long in the land.
6. You shall not kill.
7. You shall not commit adultery.
8. You shall not steal.
9. You shall not bear false witness against your neighbor.
10. You shall not covet anything that is your neighbor's.

1. You shall have no other gods before me.

In his Sermon on the Mount, Jesus gave a most useful tip to the person caught up in today's business whirl. God knows, he said, that we have need of material things—food, clothing, shelter, etc. And there is nothing wrong with desiring and attaining them. But the way we program ourselves to go about getting them *is* important. If our personal programming is defective, life's results may very well not be pleasing or even understandable to us.

His instruction is clear: "Seek first [God's] kingdom and his righteousness, and all these things shall be yours as well" (Matthew 6:33).

Jesus was merely expanding on the First Commandment: "You shall have no other gods before me."

The instruction manual at this point tells us that we should program ourselves to do what we know to be the right thing even though the *short-term* result may cost us money or even imperil our job. To do otherwise is to have a false god.

There was a banker in Kansas City named R. J. Potts whose bank failed in the Great Depression, leaving many creditors. His partner disappeared, but R. J. Potts vowed he would somehow repay all his creditors as well as his former partner's share of the obligations. Trusting in God and his righteousness, Potts formed an advertising agency. This new business prospered, and as it did, he continued to pay back all debts of his earlier business failure. For some years his family was deprived of that money, but in the *long run* he not only grew wealthy but also he possessed a warm, loving family and friends.

Because this man put God first and sought to do the right thing, God's promise to add all other things came true. When he died he was one of the city's most respected citizens.

2. You shall not worship graven images.

No doubt this commandment was a specific for the nomad Israelites as they invaded the promised land and came into contact with the more civilized Canaanite city dwellers. There they witnessed a more highly organized religion wherein carved statues and wooden symbols were worshiped as gods.

It was inevitable that this new environment would exert a glamorous attraction, almost fascination, contrasted to the austere faith of the desert-dwelling Israelites.

In the written instructions that Moses brought down from Mount Sinai, God told the Israelites that worshiping those gods made from earthen materials was a mistake. They would not profit from it.

Let us agree that the first application of this commandment was to an ancient people in an alien land. But is it not as vitally relevant to us? Witness today the near "worship" some people give to their expensive automobiles, their stereo equipment, or their homes.

Years ago, as a young insurance salesman, I wrote the homeowner's insurance for an older woman whose hobby was collecting antiques. One New Year's Eve her home was gutted by fire. All of her beautiful furniture and prized possessions were lost. The next day when I saw her she wisely said to me, "If I could give one word of advice to a younger person, it would be never allow yourself to love any inanimate objects."

It's fine to like nice things and to admire beautiful objects. But save your love for God first, and then for family and friends. Love of objects or things is a form of worshiping graven gods. Our instruction manual, the Bible, says that is a mistake.

Once I had the unpleasant task of demoting a middle manager. He was a good technician but had demonstrated that he had been promoted above his level of competence. When I broke this news to him, I expected him to be concerned primarily about the probable reduction in salary. Instead his biggest worry seemed to be that he would no longer have a private secretary. He asked plaintively, "Who will bring me my coffee?" He had been "worshiping" the trappings and privileges of his office.

3. You shall not take the name of the Lord, your God, in vain.

The Ten Commandments are among the strongest proscriptions in our manual. But this, the third one, is broken so frequently that there is now little or no social censure for doing so. Yet, I have in mind several men and women, close friends, who are hard-working, honest churchgoers with what we take to be good Christian faith. Nevertheless, they are bothered by physical ills and recurring bad luck.

One trait I have noticed that they have in common is their use of the word *God* in casual conversation. By casual I mean saying something like, "I was over at the shopping center today, and God, was it ever crowded!"

If this commandment is brought to their attention they either display vexation at being criticized or else they just shrug it off. Either way they usually continue with the habit.

Yet, there must be power in this commandment that escapes people who ignore it. If not, why would God make it one of his ten along with such serious matters as stealing and murder?

Perhaps the answer lies in the words *in vain*. One meaning of the phrase is "useless" or better yet "worthless." In this

19

•

connection, *in vain* applies to that which has no real value or meaning. If I buy a system for reducing my inventory and it fails to do so, that system has proved to be worthless and to have no real value. I have used it in vain.

One of the writers in our manual, the Bible, is the fifth century B.C. prophet Joel. Toward the end of his second chapter, he tells us how to obtain competent help if the output from our efforts in life seems wrong. He directs us simply to call upon the name of the Lord and we shall be delivered or saved from our problems.

Now you may say that is too easy—it is simplistic thinking. But the little magazine *Guideposts* (Carmel, New York 10512) each month is filled with true stories of people who did just that—they called upon the name of the Lord, and they were delivered from every sort of problem.

Perhaps if God's name is invoked repeatedly either casually or as a swear word without any thought given to him or to his power, that name may be useless to us when we really need it. Consequently, those who read this instruction, who understand what the words *in vain* mean, and then follow through, have opened for themselves a channel of communication to the most powerful partner anyone could ever acquire.

4. Remember the sabbath day, to keep it holy. Six days you shall labor, but the seventh day . . . you shall not do any work.

Hard work is still the easiest road to success. Those who achieve success know that the only place where success comes before work is in the dictionary. And Michael J. O'Connor, a noted Chicago business consultant, often tells his clients that they *maintain* their business between 9:00 A.M. and 5:00 P.M., but they *build* their business before and after those hours.

Yes, hard work is essential to material success. Why then not work all seven days of the week? Why ever take vacations? Wouldn't that be a great way to get ahead of competitors? It does seem so to some.

The instruction manual for a successful life, however, says no to these questions. Working without a break is a mistake. There are even some enlightened bosses who worry if one of their employees is working *too* hard. Perhaps they have read in the Bible the fourteenth chapter of Proverbs which states, "There is a way which seems right to a man, but its end is the way to death."

How often I have observed the accuracy of that proverb. People who work without a day for recreation and exercise are flirting with heart disease and mental problems, which, of course, can be the way to death. Similarly, they may be causing the death of a marital relationship or the loss of the love and affection of their children. Working without a break may seem right, but the Bible says it is a mistake which can cost dearly.

5. Honor your father and your mother, that your days may be long in the land.

In more primitive times, almost everything a child learned came from his parents. Childhood was of short duration, ending when the boy or girl could begin to perform useful work in the field, in the father's trade, or at home. If a young person did not respect his father and mother enough to listen to them and learn from them, his days might well be cut short.

Much of this is still true today. Most of us do learn our

basic values from our parents. But as mature individuals looking for success, what does this biblical instruction have to say to us? Actually, it can be looked at in at least two ways.

First of all, the employer we work for should certainly have our respect. Such a person need not be a father or mother figure to us, but in all but the most unusual case they undoubtedly have a good deal they can teach us.

And even if we cannot give them our full respect, by all means we should not dishonor them by running them down to others. That can only be a mistake. I don't think I have known anyone who disparaged the boss and ever reached his or her potential for success. Indeed, for many, their days were not long in that particular land!

The American writer Elbert Hubbard said in an often quoted statement on this subject: "If you work for a man, in heaven's name work for him! If he pays you wages that supply you your bread and butter, work for him—speak well of him, think well of him, stand by him and stand by the institution he represents."

To that I can only add, don't continue to work for someone or some company that you in good conscience cannot respect. Keep looking until you find one that you *can* honor so that your days there may be long and successful.

A second way to think about this commandment is to apply it to ourselves as parents. Are our morals and our actions such that our children find it natural and easy to honor us? Do they see us telling the truth even in difficult situations, or do they observe us lying to save money or to wiggle out of an uncomfortable spot?

Several years ago my wife and I were in London's Heathrow Airport coming home from a European trip. If you have been there, you know that you usually wait in long lines to check in. In the line with us was an American woman whose face had the saddest expression I think I have ever seen on anyone who wasn't actually weeping. We struck up a conversation and for some reason she told us about her trip over to London from the U.S. a few weeks earlier. Her fourteen-year-old son was with her and when she bought their tickets in New York, she had been able to get him through as under twelve years of age. Her expression brightened momentarily as she told us she had saved ninety-two dollars on his ticket.

I felt like telling her, "No, you didn't save ninety-two dollars; you simply stole it." I kept my mouth shut but I did wonder about that boy. He had seen in an unmistakable way that his mother's integrity was worth no more than ninety-two dollars and quite possibly a good deal less! How much honor would he bring to her as he grew up? Was she already having problems with him—and was that why she had that terribly sad face?

If we desire to have the honor and respect of our own children, it's important that they see us sincerely trying to honor all of the Ten Commandments.

Noah was a righteous man the Bible tells us, blameless in his generation. Because of this fact his entire family honored him. They honored him so much that even when he commenced building a huge boat on dry land, they helped him while everyone else was calling them crazy.

Noah had a wife and three sons, all of whom had wives. Isn't it unusual that not one of them scoffed at him? Not only that, but Noah and his wife were able to keep their little family together and afloat on a sea of moral decadence that had flooded their entire society.

People say we are living in immoral times today. This commandment reminds us that we, too, can keep our families afloat above the strong currents of drug abuse and sexual permissiveness by the very example of our own lives.

Our instruction manual is concerned with total family success in life—not just monetary success in business.

6. You shall not kill.

Few who read this book will ever be tempted to kill a human being. The meaning of this commandment is so plain to see that it is one of the foundations of all civilized law. But it has other applications in business.

One of the all-around successful men that I know is Robert P. Ingram, among other things the owner of two radio stations in Kansas City. One of his stations is a classical music station; except for the news and some advertisements, nothing goes over the air but the finest in great music.

Bob Ingram has had surprising success with his high quality programming. He had no real competition in this field until another station started in the area with a very similar format. For the first time, classical music lovers had a choice of stations.

Now, hardly anyone likes to see competition enter his territory, but one day after a high wind had blown over the transmitting tower of the rival station, Bob Ingram did something unusual. He called the manager of that station offering the loan of his chief engineer and his know-how to help them resume operations quickly. That is not the sort of thing you might expect in a highly competitive business.

Later Mr. Ingram was asked why he would extend all this assistance to his competitor and he replied simply, "I had what he needed to survive."

In other words, by withholding his help, Bob Ingram felt he would have been contributing to the killing of that other station.

7. You shall not commit adultery.

I believe that the majority of Americans have the good moral sense to obey this commandment. It is comforting to know that some national polls support this belief.

But this commandment makes good business sense as well. In spite of the loosening of many moral restraints, it is simply not good business to have someone advancing to top management who has little respect for the vows of marriage.

The book of Proverbs is aptly called one of the Wisdom Books. Its instructions are of a practical nature, meaning especially success in life. It is concerned with keeping the young from making mistakes out of sheer ignorance. And in those biblical days, the only young that the wisdom writers were interested in were the young men.

Proverbs 7:6-23 is interesting in what it says about the price to be paid for both adultery and what the Bible terms fornication or any extramarital sex. According to Proverbs, the price is life itself.

At the window of my house . . . I have perceived among the youths, a young man without sense, passing along the street . . . . And lo, a woman meets him. . . . With much seductive speech she persuades him. . . . All at once he follows her, as an ox goes to the slaughter, or as a stag is caught fast . . . he does not know it will cost him his life.

Now, when someone uses the phrase "It will cost you your life" that usually gets attention! But what does it mean in the modern business world?

I knew a vice president of an important West Coast firm who was on his way to the presidency of that company. Moreover, he had a beautiful wife and three loving children. His home in the country was a showplace, and he had ample space for his enclosed dog runs, because raising show dogs was his pride and joy.

But somewhere along the line he became enamored of a woman in the big city where he worked. Before long he had set her up in an apartment and was leading a double life.

It is not surprising that his adultery eventually came to light. After a time the outcome of this affair was that his wife divorced him and he lost her. He had also lost interest in the other woman, so that did not work out either. He lost much of the meaningful contact with his children, and, of course, he lost his house. Without that house he could no longer keep his dogs, and so even his cherished hobby vanished.

In a very real sense, his mistake of not following the seventh commandment did in truth cost him his former, happy life. To cap it all off, he never became president of that or any other company.

Besides causing unhappiness at home and problems with children, adultery often causes faltering energies in business—even for those with the brightest promise of success. Because of this one mistake those lives may not develop the way they should. Somewhere along the way they were lost.

8. You shall not steal.

Emmet Fox, a well-known religious philosopher and teacher earlier in this century, found it useful to substitute the words *can not* for *shall not* in many of the Ten Commandments. Thus, this statement would read, "You can not steal." Now, Emmet Fox knew that thieves *do* break through and steal and that people do cheat (which is a form of stealing), but his point was that you cannot steal and have the abundant life that Jesus promised. Stealing, he says, conflicts with fundamental law, God's law. When we give up trying to cheat and steal, God's abundance can begin to flow through us, and we shall come into our own rights.

People steal in all manners of ways. One businessman, for example, had phony business cards printed that would enable him to buy certain products at wholesale. Yet, he would undoubtedly deny vehemently that he had ever stolen anything from anyone.

Contrast his example with that of Charles L. Tivol, a Midwestern jeweler, who enjoyed the highest reputation for integrity, the kind of reputation that is indeed important for success in the jewelry business. Because most of us don't know much about precious stones, we have to rely on the word of the jeweler.

One of Charles Tivol's customers had purchased an expensive pair of pearl earrings and insured them. Not long thereafter she reported to her insurance agent that one of the large, costly pearls was missing. He instructed her to return the earring to Tivol's for its replacement and to send the bill to him. When Charles Tivol examined the earring, he seized the telephone and called the agent.

"Don't turn in that claim report," he said. "I can tell by looking at the prongs of this earring that they were not made strong enough. It is my fault the pearl was lost and I'll pay for its replacement."

To have done otherwise, he explained later, would have been to steal from the insurance company.

9. You shall not bear false witness against your neighbor.

Jim Bryson was a talented copywriter. He was hard working and he drove himself to attain success. The thought of anyone surpassing him was almost too painful for him to tolerate. So, at any meeting where he thought he could get away with it, he would carefully and subtly pass on innuendo and rumor against those whom he feared might overtake him. Often these were people who couldn't fight back—junior account people, the media buyer, his own assistant.

Bryson's strategy was based upon his own fear and insecurity. And it seemed to work—for awhile. His unquestioned creative ability carried him along for some time, but ultimately the suspicions, the lies, and the distrust that he had been sowing over the years caught up with him, and he was fired.

You see, Jim Bryson never really understood the significance that life's textbook places on this commandment. He had never focused on one of the Bible's most inflexible rules for business success, the law of retribution.

Jesus gave a succinct definition of this law in his Sermon on the Mount. He said, "Judge not, that you be not judged. For with the judgment you pronounce you will be judged, and *the measure you give will be the measure you get*" (Matthew 7:1-3, italics added).

Life does seem to have the habit of giving back to each of us what we put into it. Lies and deceits will surely catch up with us. Such rottenness will either be exposed, or we ourselves will be undone by the treachery of someone else. There is a balance to human nature as there is to physical nature. The law of gravity states that what goes up must come down. The law of retribution merely says that what goes out (from you) must come back (to you). Saying something untrue about the unpopular woman on the block or about a co-worker or even a competitor is a mistake. So is it to pass along unfounded assumptions or prejudices about a different ethnic group. Somewhere, sometime, these self-serving judgments will return to do us harm. Thus they can be classified as mistakes.

Jacob, son of Isaac and grandson of Abraham, greatly advanced himself in early manhood by means of lies and deceit. He tricked his brother, Esau, out of his birthright; he duped his dying father and cheated his brother again, this time out of their father's blessing. But remember how all that later caught up with him? He eventually had to flee for his life to his uncle, Laban. There he served his uncle for seven years in order to be allowed to marry his youngest daughter, Rachel. But Laban deceived Jacob, substituting his oldest daughter, Leah, for Rachel. In order to have Rachel as his wife, Jacob was forced to serve Laban another seven years. Fourteen years of servitude for the woman he loved. Quite a price to pay!

You'll remember also, how Jacob was later hoodwinked by his own sons who sold into slavery Joseph, the child whom Jacob loved above all others. They then showed their father Joseph's "coat of many colors" which they had dipped in the blood of a goat. Jacob believed his beloved son had been killed by a wild beast. For him the law of retribution had come full circle.

Paul, in his letter to the Galatians, said this, "Do not be deceived; God is not mocked, for whatever a man sows, that he will also reap" (6:7).

Those words could have saved Jim Bryson, the copywriter, from the garbage he put forth into life and the trashing he got back from it. But he never read the instruction manual, so he thought that he could bear false witness against others at no peril to himself. As Paul warned, Bryson was indeed deceived.

10. You shall not covet anything that is your neighbor's.

I doubt that there are many who have not at some time or another ardently desired something that belonged to another person. Keeping to the realm of business, this could mean envying the boss because of his position and his power or wishing for the wealth and the ease such wealth appears to bring a rich person. It could mean hungering for the good luck and the success that some men and women seem to meet at every turn. Always there are others more favored by "fortune and men's eyes" than we believe ourselves to be.

Should we then turn our backs to these very natural inclinations and try to convince ourselves that riches and power have little attraction for us? Such a decision in all likelihood is sheer nonsense. We would be trying to fool ourselves. It brings to mind Franklin P. Adams's little poem entitled "The Rich Man."

> *The rich man has his motor-car,*
> *His country and his town estate.*
> *He smokes a fifty-cent cigar*
> *And jeers at Fate. . . .*
>
> *Yet though my lamp burns low and dim,*
> *Though I must slave for livelihood—*
> *Think you that I would change with him?*
> *You bet I would!*

If we are to rise to the top in any business or profession it is essential that this tenth commandment not be confused with legitimate ambition. There are two underlying differences between covetousness and indispensable ambition.

Covetousness implies that God's stock of riches, power and prestige is a limited one—that there are only so much material wealth and peer acclaim to go around. So if others have already acquired much, I can only envy them and grasp for what is theirs, or otherwise I'll be left out in the cold. Money and the other trappings of success are in short supply.

Many in business undoubtedly have this mistaken view of the way God works in the world. The aim of this last commandment is to raise the level of awareness of God's unbounded creativity. How God must love to create! If you doubt this, think for a few minutes how profligate God was when he created the universe. There he was, flinging stars and planets and even whole galaxies across space like a millionaire spendthrift throwing away money. Only God never diminished his supply. The farther we are able to peer into space, the more galactic nebulae are discovered. Do they go on forever? Is God still strewing other milky ways through unknown skies? Whatever he may be doing, we know this—his lavishness knows no measure.

One acre of vacant land may contain more insects than there are people in the United States. Botanists have been studying grasses and weeds for many years, but they have not yet been able to categorize them all.

Why such profusion? The answer is clear. Do you burn with ambition? Splendid, I say. Just don't waste time thinking of what others have achieved. Direct your energies, instead, to selling more effectively, or to producing more efficiently, or to increasing your knowledge and your skills—in short, to serving others better. Thus you will open wide a channel to God's absolutely unlimited resources. And, without coveting, you too can satisfy your ambition and gain the desired reward.

Sometimes we will grant that God's supply is inexhaustible. But we may say, "My ambition is to become head of this department, or of this division, or even of this entire company. But I am trapped in this job by those over me. They are not close to retirement, and they are quite capable.

Therefore, since I covet their positions, I may just think up a few sly ways to discredit them so I can take their positions away from them."

The instruction manual tells us that to covet is always a mistake. Garbage in, garbage out. Covetousness has no place in true ambition. The wise know that the future is not really under our control. Of course, we should prepare to advance ourselves, but it is God who sets our agenda, and he is free to set it in any way or manner he chooses.

One of the differences between the so-called false prophets and the great prophets of the Old Testament rests upon this very point. The false prophets said in effect that the God who chose the Hebrews, who led them out of Egypt, and who gave them the promised land would defend them and never let them be taken out of it regardless of whether or not they obeyed his commandments.

The true prophets, however, warned against such an attempt to box God in. They cautioned that the God who chose them and who led them and who supplied all their needs was indeed also free to take them from their lands if he so decided. And, of course, decide he did and out they went into captivity for a period of time.

Do you remember Jesus' parable of the wise and foolish virgins? When they went to await the bridegroom's arrival, the five foolish maidens took no oil for their lamps. They apparently thought there would be plenty of time later on for them to buy the oil to light their lamps. But when he arrived at midnight, they were unprepared. Consequently, they were denied admittance to the marriage feast.

The above examples are there to tell us that the future is not ours to control. While we can and should prepare ourselves for opportunities, we must not waste our energies coveting anything of others. Instead, we should through prayer keep ourselves open to God's timetable for us. That could well prove to be more exciting than anything we might be plotting or scheming about in our own finite minds.

This is a moral law—of such consequence that God chose to include it as the last of his ten great commandments.

Chapter Three

A BALANCING ACT
How to Keep Sane Under Pressure

From the cowardice *that shrinks from new truth,*
From the laziness *that is content with half-truth,*
From the arrogance *that thinks it knows all truth,*
O God of Truth, deliver us.

Ancient Prayer

The man or woman on the road to business or professional success can further his or her progress on that happy road by keeping this fine, old prayer in mind. Why? Because the three common mistakes it mentions lead to what is often called a closed mind. That kind of a mind in an executive often brings on problems. And here's why.

A mind that is closed, whether from cowardice, laziness, or arrogance, cannot be considered a balanced mind. And long-term success is more easily achieved by those who have such balance.

We read a great deal about the pressures that managers and executives are subjected to. The knowledge that their decisions often change the future for other people weighs on their minds. The same can be said for physicians, lawyers, and politicians—all of whom take on grave responsibilities and face tough choices. At such times the pressures can indeed run high.

Under pressure, cowardly minds do close so as not to have to face bewildering new information—a tragic mistake. Also, under pressure we often go ahead with decisions without digging for sufficient information. If we're lucky, the decisions may prove to be acceptable solutions to the problems, but perhaps not the *best* ones we could have devised had we not been lazy and content with partial truth. If unlucky, then chalk up another mistake.

As for arrogance, of course, that kind of pride in our own superiority has long been recognized as one of the mistakes or factors often involved in financial failures. There are many causes of arrogance. One of them is, again, pressure. The pressure of trying to hold onto our title or position.

This can lead, as a defense, to the development of an overbearing manner. Such people haughtily assert their superior importance. They are saying in effect, "I know what is best. You keep a low profile and don't make any waves around me (or you might upset my canoe!)."

So how does the instruction manual guide us in coping with intense pressure? What are its directives for maintaining a balanced mind so that we can avoid the three errors or sins of shrinking from new truth—being content with half-truth and haughtily claiming to be right in all that we do?

The Bible contains numerous recitations of how pressure inflamed and destroyed the minds of different characters throughout the history that it encompasses. One of the best known examples is the modern-as-today story of Saul, the first king of Israel.

At the beginning of the story as told in First Samuel, Saul was an impressive young man. He possessed kingly physical attributes. The biblical account says, "There was not a man among the people of Israel more handsome than he; from his shoulders upward he was taller than any of the people" (9:2). He was brave in battle and courageous in all of his actions. Saul was earnestly trying to do the best job he could in governing Israel. He sought to do God's will, at least at the beginning.

But then David came onto the scene and Saul began to

think less about governing well under God and more about keeping his crown. He realized that David's popularity among the people was becoming greater than his own. He worried about the very real possibility that David might wrest the throne from him, especially after he heard some women singing, "Saul has slain his thousands and David his ten thousands" (18:7).

Saul's mind became unbalanced. The pressures he felt took a terrific toll on him. He no longer was devoted to what was best for his country, and from here on his course was all downhill until the day he died upon his own sword.

In matters of balance, a person's mind can be compared to an automobile engine. If the engine is unbalanced or out of tune, speeding up its revolutions (applying pressure) will likely cause it to quiver and tremble. Indeed, if the pressure on it continues, the vibration may shake it to pieces, and it will either blow apart or just stop.

On the other hand, a well-balanced engine welcomes pressure. It can be "revved up" to very high speeds without faltering. Pressure applied on its throttle delivers a smooth, eager response. *There is no strain.*

In like manner there are executives who thrive on pressure. Their minds (and bodies) flourish under stress. They somehow learned how to keep it all in balance even when others are falling apart.

Here are two good ways to keep your mind balanced, in tune, and able to respond positively to pressures.

There can be no substitute for knowledge and ability. When the executive has worked hard to acquire the requisite learning and skills, he can handle the pressures of management and decision making.

Let me ask you a question. How would you like to have to

face an uninterested and bored audience—*and* be expected to make them laugh? I don't know about you, but I can imagine the unbearable strain I would feel in that situation. I would probably fall apart because I do not have the skill to do that kind of work. I have not studied for it. I have not practiced long hours telling jokes or singing funny songs. I do not have the craftsmanship that is required. But let me recount how easy it was to do just that for someone who *did* have both the necessary ability and the years of hard work and practice to put it over.

Some years ago before I was married I was in San Francisco on a business trip. I telephoned a young woman I knew in Monterey, California, a drive of a couple of hours. I asked her for a dinner date later in the week. She said fine but added that we would be with some others, one of whom would be Danny Kaye. Well, of course, I was delighted. Danny Kaye was at the peak of his popularity then, which, as you know, has lasted a long time.

We met and went to a restaurant near the old Del Monte Hotel. The dining room was on the main floor, and there was a wide staircase leading to a large banquet hall on the second floor.

As we were seated in the dining room, Danny Kaye was in a serious mood. He said, "I have just finished a two-week engagement at the Palace Theatre in San Francisco and for that I was paid more than three hundred thousand dollars. I just wonder," he continued, "if I could possibly be worth that amount."

At that point a little man came down the stairway and to our table. He was obviously nervous, but he said, "Mr. Kaye, I am the program chairman of the Monterey Lions Club. We're having our annual Sweethearts' Dinner upstairs. All of our wives are here and the entertainment that we hired has failed to show up. We're all just sitting up there, not saying anything, and the dinner is a total failure. Now, Mr. Kaye, we couldn't begin to afford your price, but if you could find it in your heart to come stick your head in the doorway and just say, 'hello folks,' that would give them something to talk about. They would say, 'Who was that? Was that really Danny Kaye?' and that might salvage the evening."

Without hesitation Danny said, "Of course," and he started for the stairs. I grabbed my date and followed, dying to see what this great entertainer would do.

When we opened the door to that large room you never saw such a dismal looking group of people. Talk about a cold audience! I was chilled by just looking at them. But Danny Kaye was relaxed and confident.

Within thirty seconds he had them chuckling, and within a minute we were all laughing so hard I had to lean against a wall to keep from falling. Calling upon his huge reservoir of talent, he cracked a few jokes and sang one or two hilarious ditties. Then at that point a waitress with a tray balanced above her head burst through a swinging door. Danny took one look at her and had the ability to surmise that she was Irish. So he spoke to her in a perfect Irish brogue, having mastered many dialects. To the delight of all, she replied in one.

He put down her tray, and they danced an Irish jig while he hummed the tune. People were collapsing with laughter all over the room. I suppose we were in there no more than ten minutes, but as we walked back, the laughter from that room rolled down the stairs like a mighty river, flooding the downstairs where the rest of the guests sat in puzzled silence.

I thought to myself, this man has just done an impossible thing. And he did it easily, with no apparent strain. So, as we sat down again I leaned over to him and said from the admiration in my heart, "Mr. Kaye, any man who can do what you just did is worth every cent the Palace Theatre paid you!"

The point here, of course, is that there can be no substitute for knowledge and ability. The executive who continues to improve both his knowledge and his management skills will have gone a long way toward maintaining a balanced mind.

The second procedure for acquiring such balance is twofold. First, please *look up and read* in your manual the following verses:

1. Isaiah 42:16   —I will lead the blind in a way that they know not . . .
2. Isaiah 43:2   —When you pass through the waters I will be with you . . .
3. Isaiah 30:20-23   —And though the Lord give you the bread of adversity . . .
4. Isaiah 59:1   —Behold, the Lord's hand is not shortened, that it cannot save . . .
5. Isaiah 54:14-17   —In righteousness you shall be established . . .
6. Joshua 1:5   —As I was with Moses . . .
7. Matthew 6:33   —But seek first his kingdom . . .
8. Psalm 91:1, 2   —He who dwells in the shelter . . .
9. Psalm 118:5, 6   —Out of my distress . . .
10. Proverbs 1:33   —He who listens to me will dwell secure . . .
11. Proverbs 3:5, 6   —Trust in the Lord with all your heart . . .
12. Proverbs 16:3   —Commit your work to the Lord . . .

Do you see the theme that runs through them? Perhaps an explanation of number 6 will serve for all.

You'll recall what a magnificent leader Moses had been to his people. There never had been one to equal his deeds. God performed miracle after miracle through him. Here is one good example.

After the travail of escaping the slavery in Egypt, there was Moses encamped with his people on the shore of what may have been the Red Sea. The people of Israel lifted up their eyes, and behold, the Egyptians were marching after them, and they were in great fear. And they said to Moses, "Is it because there are no graves in Egypt that you have taken us away to die in the wilderness? . . . It would have been better for us to serve the Egyptians than to die in the wilderness" (14:11-12).

It is difficult to imagine a situation where a leader could be under greater pressure than this! In front of Moses lay a great body of water and he had no boats; to the rear, a huge well-trained army was racing after him and he had no arms; to cap it all, his people in their panic were blaming him for their mortal danger.

Moses knew their predicament was desperate. But he did not falter under the strain. God had brought them this far, and Moses was confident that God does not mock his children. He would not forsake them now when escape lay just across that sea.

So Moses turned to his people and spoke these stirring words, "Fear not, stand firm, and see the salvation of the Lord, which he will work for you today" (14:13). Then he prayed. And God said to Moses, "Lift up your rod, and stretch out your hand over the sea and divide it, that the people of Israel may go on dry ground through the sea" (14:16).

Of course they were saved, as everyone knows. This is one

of the most familiar of all of the thrilling accounts of God's power in the Bible.

Eventually, Moses grew very old and died. God then chose Joshua to lead this wandering band of Israelites, to be their new chief executive. Taking over after such a leader as Moses must have been a frightening prospect for Joshua. Many centuries later another leader, Harry Truman, was stunned by the fact that he was now to take the reins of government from our long-term president, Franklin Delano Roosevelt.

The day after Roosevelt's death in 1945, President Truman said to reporters, "When they told me yesterday what had happened, I felt like the moon, the stars, and all the planets had fallen on me."

So it probably was with Joshua. But the Lord gave him this remarkable pledge. He said, "As I was with Moses, so I will be with you; I will not fail you or forsake you" (1:5). Joshua then bravely took command and discovered that God indeed amply fulfilled that promise.

Returning now to the plan for developing a balanced mind, here is the hardest part of it for many of us. How can we be certain that such a promise by God, made some thousands of years ago, is equally valid for us today? There is no question, is there, that God was speaking to just one person, Joshua? Wasn't it just the particular circumstance of his assuming leadership at one specific time and place in biblical history?

The answer to those questions is that we can't be *absolutely* sure of anything! But, men and women of faith over the centuries have come to believe that the Bible is, as we sometimes say, Everyman's Book. That simply means that our universal experience has demonstrated over and over again for countless individuals that the promises of God in the Bible are true for all people of all races for all of time.

Admittedly this is impossible to prove by intellectual

reasoning. What *is* needed is enough faith or trust to test these promises for ourselves. The next time you are faced with a problem, think of God saying to you, "As I was with Moses, so I will be with you."

It is good to recall the many problems that both Moses and Joshua faced, and how God helped them solve them all. It doesn't hurt, either, to remind God of this particular promise. Then claim his invincible help for yourself. With a little practice, this can come quite easily. You will be the judge of the results.

More than a hundred generations have tested this pledge. If it, along with many others, had not been fulfilled, the Bible would not remain at the top of the best-sellers' list year after year!

So, to summarize, remember to avoid the three mistakes of that old prayer at the beginning of this chapter. Keep your mind in balance by strengthening your business skills, and lastly, step out in faith to claim the promises of God for your own.

Chapter Four

GETTING THROUGH GIVING
The Rewards of Tithing

It would be both interesting and illuminating if the thoughts of those reading this chapter could be examined. For many of us, a concept which states that generous giving brings generous rewards seems to go against our common sense. Your first reaction to such a statement may very well be a mixture of skepticism and rejection, but bear with me, at least to the extent of reading the whole chapter!

The rejection of the idea of liberal giving could well be *the* principal reason that there is so much worry and stress over financial security in our country today. In 1984, a *Reader's Digest*/Gallup Survey representing a cross section of the general population reported that 23 percent of the adults interviewed said they "always" or "nearly always" have difficulty meeting their monthly expenses. Another 27 percent said they "frequently" have such problems. That would indicate that exactly one-half of our adult population lives with definite money worries.

Some things that seem unbelievable at first, upon closer inspection, may actually turn out to be true. Life is full of paradoxes. For example, contemporary philosophy says that we only go around once in life so, therefore, we should strive for all of the happiness we can get. And yet, the major religions of the world teach that if a person lives selfishly and chases happiness, he will become the most miserable of all persons.

Our handbook, the Bible, says that we should repay no one evil for evil, but to take thought instead of what is noble. Such a statement seems impractical. It goes against our grain. And yet, when given a trial it usually works. There was a story reported in a magazine years ago of a young soldier in boot camp who read his Bible every night sitting on the edge of his bunk. This irritated one of the other recruits, who, spoiling for a fight, tore the Bible from his hands, ripped out some of its pages, and threw it into a corner.

The young soldier did not respond as expected. He retrieved his Bible without saying a word and calmly went to bed. But during the night he arose and cleaned and polished the bully's muddy boots. When the latter awakened the next morning and saw what had been done, he wept.

Do you know that there are many biblical passages that promise material blessings to those who give away 10 percent or more of their income (tithe)? Such promises may be difficult to believe, I know. You see, they too are paradoxes.

One of the best known of God's promises regarding giving is Malachi 3:10, which speaks of giving away 10 percent of income: "Bring the full tithes into the storehouse . . . and thereby put me to the test, says the Lord of hosts, if I will not open the windows of heaven for you and pour down for you an overwhelming blessing."

Other examples:

"Honor the Lord with . . . the first fruits of all your produce; then your barns will be filled with plenty" (Proverbs 3:9).

"One man gives freely, yet grows all the richer; another withholds what he should give, and only suffers want" (Proverbs 11:24, 25).

"The point is this: he who sows sparingly will also reap sparingly, and he who sows bountifully will also reap bountifully" (II Corinthians 9:6).

"If you keep the commandments of the Lord your God . . . the Lord will make you abound in prosperity" (Deuteronomy 28:9, 11).

Of all of the commandments of God (not just the Ten Commandments), this one on tithing is one of the most troublesome. How can the prayer of Saint Francis possibly be more than a beautiful, pious thought when he declares, "For it is in giving that we receive"? Our worldly common sense asks how can that be? We might not say so in words, but we show clearly by our actions that we believe all that to be utter nonsense.

How do you suppose this practice of giving away at least one-tenth of income developed in the first place? It appears to have had ancient beginnings. The oldest of the world's principal continuing religions is Hinduism. Its origin has been lost in the mists of time. But one of the Hindu proverbs coming down through the centuries asserts, "They who give have all things. They who withhold have nothing."

It is not at all strange that the Hindus should have this saying. Nearly all religious systems warn against our very natural desire to grasp for all of the material wealth we can get, and then to clasp it tightly to ourselves. Paul Pruyser, in his book *A Dynamic Psychology of Religion*, has written, "Religions have advocated time and again the idea of stewardship in order to regulate man's attitude toward things, especially possessions" (Harper & Row, 1968).

The genesis of this idea of giving back a portion of what we get may have begun more than ten thousand years ago.

Primitive man was primarily a hunter. His tribe was nomadic, moving to wherever there was game. But about 8000 B.C. the tribal society began systematically to gather wild berries and grains in addition to hunting for food. Over time they noticed that new crops of wild grain usually came up again the next season in the same fields as before. And then they made their big discovery. The crops sprang back because of the seeds that had been accidentally dropped during the previous gathering.

They learned by observation that the more they let slip through their fingers during the harvest, the more there would be for them the next year!

Those people were now able to give up their nomadic ways and live together in one place. This led eventually to village life. But such was not possible if they kept everything to themselves.

A dedicated Jewish rabbi and scholar of note, William B. Silverman, has said that there is no doubt that tithing is an ancient practice and that the tithe meant one-tenth. For example, Abraham's meeting with the shadowy figure of Melchizedek is intriguing because the latter is called "Priest of God Most High," and Abraham feels the need to give him a tenth of all that he had gained in battle (Genesis 14:18-20).

In the book of Leviticus, God himself makes a claim on what we produce. "All the tithe of the land, whether of the seed of the land or the fruit of the trees, is the Lord's . . . and all the tithe of herds and flocks, every tenth animal . . . shall be holy to the Lord" (27:30, 32). There can hardly be a more succinct directive.

"Well!" you may say. "All of that is fine for a primitive society. But does it work today? That's the key question."

My answer, for which I shall try to show proof, is yes! Yes, it does indeed work. It works so well that I think of it as a law—the law of tithing. During the past few years, I have been doing a bit of public speaking and traveling some around the country. In my talks, I have often mentioned the importance of tithing and have never yet had anyone disagree *who has tried it*. Almost always, at the end of the speech, one or more from the audience will take a moment to affirm to me that what I said about tithing has proven to be true in their lives.

The only exception was a sad looking man I sat next to in an airport limousine leaving a conference center in Scottsdale, Arizona. I mentioned my talk on tithing, which he had not heard.

He exclaimed with some passion, "I tried tithing for a whole year, and I'll never do that again."

"What happened?" I asked anxiously. "Did your business lose money, or did some investments go sour?"

"Oh, no," he replied, "nothing like that, but that was the year my son died."

Of course, I expressed my sympathy and let the matter drop. It was apparent that in his search for some reason for his son being taken from him he had seized on this one recent change he had made in his own pattern of giving, and he blamed it for his son's death. That surely is a preposterous judgment, but I mention it because it is the only adverse opinion I have encountered in this matter of tithing.

Gordon Groth, the former president of Electra Manufacturing Company, once said that he had known many regular churchgoers who, for one reason or another, quit going to church, but he had never found anyone who ever stopped tithing once they had established the practice. His comment was that they were afraid to stop—afraid, because their tithing had brought them increased material blessings, which they felt would disappear if they ever discontinued it.

William Volker, the inventor of the roll-up window shade, gave away enormous amounts of money. While still a comparatively young man he was worth several million dollars. He and his wife decided they would keep one million and give away all above that amount.

Now that's one profound decision for anyone to make! Many of his friends thought he had taken leave of his senses. In fact, one of those friends said to him much later, "Bill, I was sure you would end up in a pauper's grave, but here you are, richer than ever, in spite of all that money you have been shoveling out for years."

William Volker replied, "Yes, I have been shoveling it out, but God has been shoveling more of it right back to me, and God has a bigger shovel."

His story is impressive, no doubt, but it does not constitute proof of the validity of the law of tithing. In 1978 I determined to seek proof by going to the Gallup Organization in Princeton, New Jersey, and discussing this question with Arthur L. Keiser, who was then president. He agreed to include my questions on tithing in one of the regular Gallup surveys, which sample the opinions of the American people.

You might be interested in knowing a little about how the Gallup Organization conducts its polls. They use what is called the "Scientific Survey" method. About fifteen hundred persons across the nation are interviewed. They have been selected to produce an approximation of the adult civilian population, eighteen years and older, in all socioeconomic groups.

The personal interviews are conducted when adults are most likely at home. Unless they state otherwise no telephone contacts or mail-in questionnaires are used. The questions asked are on all manner of subjects. In this particular survey, my questions were mixed in with perhaps two hundred and fifty others on various subjects. My three questions, therefore, would not have attracted particular attention:

Question 1: Do you personally give one-tenth or more of your income to a church or charity?

Question 2: Do you personally know anyone who does give one-tenth or more of his or her income to a church or charity?

Question 3: If your answer to question 2 was yes, do those people who give one-tenth or more have serious financial problems or not?

Most people are surprised at the results of the poll. To question number one, 22 percent of the persons interviewed said that they do give one-tenth or more of their income to a church or charity. Think of that! More than one out of every five persons tithed.

The answers to question 2 were even more amazing:

Do you personally know anyone who does give one-tenth or more of his or her income to a church or charity?

Those answering yes	46 percent
Those answering no	53 percent
Don't know	1 percent
	100 percent

Nearly half the American people (based upon this sample) said they know someone who gives this much away. That should gladden the hearts of all fund raisers!

But the key question by all odds was the third, asked only of that 46 percent who said they did know someone who gave 10 percent: Do those people who give one-tenth or more have serious financial problems or not?

Their replies reveal the power of this law of tithing. First of all, there were 15 percent who could not answer the question. They frankly just did not know anything about the financial status of their friends or relatives who tithed. And that is easy to understand.

Of those remaining who could answer the question, 13 percent replied that the tithers they knew did seem to have financial problems, but a whopping 87 percent said NO, they did not have those kinds of problems.

To find such a large number of Americans in agreement on any subject is not only unusual but most exciting. That's especially true on this type of subject. The conclusion is inescapable. The American people, who had reason to know, believed in June of 1978 that the odds are extremely good (87-13) that the biblical promises regarding tithing continue to be valid in these modern times. Prosperity, or at least the lack of serious money worries, occurs with the use of this law of tithing.

There still remains, however, one essential question to be answered. How much self-control is needed to become a tither and take advantage of these odds? Well, I'm not long on self-discipline myself, and I'll show you now the only way I could have managed to have done it since hearing Gordon Groth make that statement about tithers back in 1949. There are five steps:

1. Resolve to make a fair test. Many couples who decide to tithe give it a go for a one-year period, and then evaluate it. I really doubt if a shorter period would be long enough to prove or disprove whether it works for you.

2. Resolve in your own mind that it is altogether good and proper to test God on his promises. Over the years I've had a few people challenge me on this point after one of my speeches. I referred them, and I refer you, to both the Lord's statement in the book of Malachi quoted earlier in this chapter, and to the wonderful story of Gideon's testing of God in Judges 6:36-40. You remember, God spoke directly to Gideon, performed a minor miracle to prove who he was, and then told him to deliver Israel from the Midianites. Yet, after all of that, Gideon was still uncertain of what he should do, so he tested the Lord with a fleece of wool, not once, but twice! Three tests in all, and yet God's anger did not burn against Gideon.

3. Let's assume you have one checking account wherein you deposit your paycheck and any other income from whatever sources. The next step is to open a second checking account, preferably in another bank (so that there can be no confusion between the two accounts).

4. Recognizing that the law of tithing may not work *at all* at any percentage figure below 10 percent, apply this percentage to every bank deposit you make into your regular bank account. By this, I mean, when you deposit your paycheck (and any other income check) immediately write out a check on that account to your other bank for 10 percent of that deposit. Endorse the check, and send it with a deposit slip to your other bank account.

It is at this point that one of the miracles of tithing occurs. If you make the 10 percent deposit in the second bank account instantly, you will soon realize that you do not miss it. Furthermore, at the end of the test period, the odds are very high that you will be better off financially than you are now. But you can't wait even until the end of the month to tithe, or the chances are your resolve will fail.

5. At the outset it is quite important to decide just what is and what is not income for the purpose of tithing. For example, a check you receive as repayment of a loan is obviously not income so is not subject to the tithe. Income from a farm should be treated as a sole proprietorship and tithed on the net before taxes.

   If you are lucky enough to receive an inheritance, remember in biblical times they tithed only on the produce of the land, not the land itself. So treat the inheritance in the same way, tithing only on the revenue it brings to you.

   Each tither must determine what he will consider to be tithable income. Here are some suggested items of such income:

   Salary and commissions
   Bonuses and profit sharing
   Dividends
   Interest received
   Employer's share of a stock purchase plan
   Director's fees
   Pensions—annuities—Social Security checks

A question often asked is, "Am I not expected to give all 10 percent to a church or temple?" Let's go back to the Bible again. There may well have been more than one tithe—each for a different purpose. Dr. Silverman contends that tithes originally were both for the priests and the poor. It was the duty of the priests to share those gifts with the poor, and in so doing, they also served God.

We also know that the priests or rabbis were in all probability the most educated men in their villages or towns. They were supported by the offerings of the villagers, but they provided all manner of instruction and counseling to their people in addition to their religious duties. Indeed, the word *rabbi* means teacher.

In deciding how much of your second bank account will go to your church and how much to other charities, you are urged to give and give generously to the church of your choice. If you love your church, you will be generous. It has been said that you can give without loving, but you can't love without giving. Our love of God is best expressed perhaps by our gifts to the church. But I don't think he wants us to neglect our absolutely vital charities and cultural institutions.

At one time I was the chairman of a business employing six hundred people. We were striving to become a "Fair Share" giving firm in the annual United Way Campaign. I had an associate who often frustrated me. He was a spiritual man who gave 20 percent or more of his income to his church. But he steadfastly refused to give even one dollar to the United Way, or to anything else. It was impossible to quarrel with his religious devotion, but his stubborn refusal to help anyone else in the community was a source of irritation.

The five steps I've cited will give you most of the answers that will make tithing an easy and natural part of your life-style. Do you believe that? Well, I am told by downhill skiers that when you make a turn coming down a mountain you must lean out away from the side of the mountain. Now I find that hard to believe. But then, I've never tried skiing. Nevertheless, I'm certain that my instinct or common sense would tell me to lean *in* towards the slope. In an automobile I always lean in the direction I'm turning, and I would expect to do the same while skiing. Consequently, in skiing I doubtless would fall, demonstrating again that there are some things that seem unbelievable but which when tested prove to be true after all.

If you give tithing an honest trial, you should notice at least three results in addition to increased material wealth. People normally speak of giving as an unselfish act, but the effects of tithing are very much in your own self-interest.

First of all, during the one-year period your recognition within your community should begin to increase. When a person feels an obligation to part *regularly* with some of his income in order to improve the conditions of his town or city, that fact alone in time will weave itself into the pattern of his reputation. Quite likely in the past you gave only under pressure from others and then, probably, you tried to get by with as little as possible. Isn't that standard operating procedure?

But now, the money in your second bank account is already gone, as far as you are concerned. You are not going to spend any of it on yourself or family. So, your focus from here on is simply where to send it to do the most good. That makes quite a difference. The person soliciting you recognizes you as a cheerful giver. You have heard that God loves a cheerful giver; well, so do all of us who volunteer our time to raise the monies needed to keep churches open, colleges going, and symphonies playing. We'll love and respect you for your willingness to help.

A second benefit you'll discover in tithing is the financial discipline it creates. One of the reasons, perhaps, that God's material blessings do pour down upon the tither is the training that comes automatically with setting aside 10 percent of each income check. If you do this for a year, you'll find a spillover of benefits into other areas of your budgeting. You'll have formed a valuable, tough-minded habit to apply to the control of other aspects of your spending. Financial success usually is built upon a well-regulated life. Tithing helps foster that.

Finally, the third benefit is simply the joy that will positively flow into your life. Many do not know that it is fun to give. It is especially pleasurable and easy to do when we know we can afford it. With tithing the money is there.

One of the unhappiest lives I have observed since the end of World War II was a man who had never experienced the fun of giving.

In 1950 he was barely making ends meet. I urged him to tithe, but he scornfully replied, "It's all very well for you to talk about tithing, but on the salary I'm making I can't afford to give anything. I desperately need every cent."

A few years later he had become a successful salesman and he told me proudly that during the past year he had earned $40,000.

"Splendid," I cried, "now you *can* afford to tithe."

"What?" he nearly screamed. "Give away $4,000? You must be crazy!"

Today he is divorced, alienated from his children, and still struggling financially. Giving and happiness go hand-in-hand.

So there you have it. Tithers enjoy an enhanced reputation, greater determination, and, best of all, the joy and delight in being freed from the stress of money worries.

Two thousand years ago, Jesus stated the fundamental truth of tithing. As reported by Luke, he said, "Give, and it will be given to you; good measure, pressed down, shaken together, running over, will be put into your lap. For the measure you give will be the measure you get back" (6:38).

Evangelist Billy Graham, in his daily newspaper column, has often said essentially the same thing. Several times he has said in effect, "I dare you to try to outgive God."

That is the challenge I now dare you to test!

Chapter Five

BUILDING A CODE OF ETHICS

There can be no final truth in ethics . . .
until the last man has had his experience
and said his say.

William James

As William James, the American psychologist and philosopher, said, ethics and morals do indeed change over time. As an example, when my mother was a girl at the turn of the century, her parents would not permit her to have a date after sundown without a chaperone. What a drastic change from today's morality!

Most of us use the terms *ethics* and *morals* interchangeably. Basically, they mean the same. The word *morals* comes from the Latin word *mores* meaning "custom"; *ethics* comes from the Greek word *ēthickē*, which also means "custom."

There is a subtle difference between those two words, however. A code of ethics most generally refers to a business or profession. A moral code, on the other hand, usually has to do with personal conduct. We say that Mary Jones is a very moral person meaning that she is good in character and conduct. We might refer to her husband, Bill, as an ethical lawyer because of his high professional standards in his legal practice. It would sound just a little strange to reverse those terms, especially describing Bill as a moral lawyer.

Ethics, unlike morals, can be changed instantly by the stroke of a pen. Take the ethics of the legal profession: before

1978 it was both unethical and illegal for a lawyer to advertise for clients. A lawyer doing so certainly could not belong to the American Bar Association. Subsequently, the Supreme Court and then various states amended the law to permit advertising within certain restraints. Suddenly, it was ethical within limits for a lawyer to run ads in newspapers or to appear on TV.

Morals, on the other hand, change slowly in a society. Such change often is accompanied by great trauma. As an illustration, let's go back to Mary and Bill Jones for a moment. We said that Mary is a moral person and Bill an ethical lawyer. But suppose Bill and Mary are not married and are living together in a common-law arrangement. We know what the Bible says about that sort of thing and, therefore, many would question whether they could be considered moral persons. But if Bill continued to conduct his law practice on the same high level, he, no doubt, would retain his ethical reputation.

Now as to the trauma involved in this. If you are the parent of a daughter who insists that some of your moral standards are outdated and that her moral code is going to be quite different, then you will agree there often are shock, dismay, and frustration associated with changing morals.

Sometimes in social gatherings the conversation lags. The next time you are searching for something to say to an interesting dinner companion, you might ask, "Can an ethical person in business be immoral in his or her personal life?" For my own part, I would say quite possibly.

Then, just to keep things going, ask the next question. "Can a moral person in his or her personal life be unethical in business dealings?" Not as likely, I would say.

Although there is no clear-cut distinction between these

two words, when we use them we know what we mean. Usually, there is no misunderstanding of the terms.

However, misunderstanding can lead to unintended results. Some years ago, coming home from Europe on the *S. S. Rotterdam*, I met a charming fellow, a lawyer named Ronald Sanders from a Southeastern city. As a prominent attorney, Sanders sometimes advised other lawyers who asked for his help.

One afternoon he received a telephone call from a young prosecuting attorney he knew. This young man was handling a case involving a farm girl who had accused the defendant of rape. The trial was the very next morning, and the inexperienced prosecutor was feeling somewhat panicky.

My friend, Sanders, agreed to meet with him. He said, "If you and the plaintiff," whom I'll just call Daisy May, "will come to my office in an hour, I'll go over the case with you and we'll stay there as late as necessary to get you prepared."

When the lawyer and Daisy May arrived, Sanders soon realized he had a problem. Daisy May used crude, earthy language to describe what had happened to her. Finally he had to say, "Now look, Daisy May, tomorrow you're going to be in a dignified court of law and you must not say those words when you have to tell about this incident. Instead, I want you to use the words, *sexual intercourse*, and nothing else." Sanders had her practice using those words until finally he was satisfied she would not slip.

Early the next morning they met in court, and the prosecutor led Daisy May through her testimony. To Sanders's delight she was letter-perfect. She never slipped once. Sanders felt confident.

Then it was the defense attorney's turn to cross-examine her. His opening question was, "Daisy May, when did you first learn about sexual intercourse?"

Quick as a flash she replied, "Last night in Mr. Sanders's office."

It had to be explained to Daisy May why everyone was laughing so hard that the judge declared a recess. She had completely misunderstood the question.

I will guess that you have read the Bible. You may, in fact, have established a daily reading habit. Even so, unless you have guidance, you may not clearly understand the scriptural message regardng business ethics. I know I didn't until I completed six semesters of graduate work in the Department of Religious Studies at the University of Kansas. What follows is distilled from lecture notes taken and books read in those various courses.

Those who have majored in philosophy know that traditionally philosophers have asked the question, "What is man's chief good?" This is an abstract concept. Biblical ethics, on the other hand, is more concerned with "What is the *right* thing for a man to do in any given situation?"

For the Hebrews, God, or Jehovah, was not a metaphysical entity whose existence could be debated; rather, they saw him as the instigating force behind all actual worldly events.

The ethical code in the Bible is characterized by its practicality. It concentrates on those acts that affect one's neighbor. The books of Leviticus and Deuteronomy are full of admonitions of this sort. They range from the proper treatment of creditors, the poor, the wife of a neighbor, to even the stranger who was in their midst.

It is not so much the abstruse ideal of love, but how love should be acted out toward others; not so much the ideal of truth, but truthfulness toward others.

"You shall not steal, nor deal falsely, nor lie to one another. . . . The wages of a hired servant shall not remain with you all night. . . . You shall not curse the deaf or put a stumbling block before the blind. . . . You shall have just balances, just weights. . . . And you shall observe all my statutes and all my ordinances, and do them: I am the Lord" (Leviticus 19:11, 13, 14, 36, 37).

As you can see there is great emphasis upon justice. "Justice, and only justice, you shall follow" (Deuteronomy 16:20). The code demands that you determine what is the just thing to do for all involved. The present day Four-way test of Rotary International reads very much in this vein. It says in part, "Will [my action] be fair to all concerned? Will it be beneficial to all concerned?"

Jesus, in his time, and Paul, a little later, infused fresh inspiration into the older code. Our ethics and actions are now to be based, they said, on what God has already given us. Think of God's love, his forgiveness and mercy; also, keep in mind the material possessions and good health that are ours. These come from God. Therefore, according to the New Testament, ethical conduct should not deny such blessings to others. We do this in business and in our personal lives not just to win God's favor but in rejoicing, because he has already given them to us—in most cases abundantly.

Let's see how appreciation for God's gifts fits into a modern business code of ethics. His love, forgiveness, and mercy can be considered together. If an employer is aware of God's love for all of his children, he will not deny an advancement to an employee because of race, color, sex, or creed. He will do his best to rid himself of all prejudices in order to deal fairly with those under his supervision.

Such an employer or manager will not manage by fear techniques, but more along the lines of McGregor's Theory Y, or the Japanese Quality Circles idea. Thus he will be able to foster positive feedback up and down the chain of command, increasing both the morale and the productivity of his people.

It has been charged that there is much plotting to get even with others in the business world—the idea of revenge against someone. Actually, I have seen very little of this. I believe I observed about as much in my three years in academia as I did in thirty years of competitive business.

But we do know that lawsuits are increasing, and more and more plaintiffs are asking for punitive awards. Such awards are meant to punish the defendant by seeking additional damages from him as a means of revenge. Unless you hark back to the very early and primitive "an eye for an eye and a tooth for a tooth" sort of ethics, it is difficult to reconcile many of these lawsuits with the forgiveness and mercy of God.

I do like the story of President Lincoln who once overruled the death sentence given to a very young soldier who had fled from his first encounter with the enemy. In his official pardon of the lad, Lincoln wrote, "I have observed that it does not do a boy much good to shoot him."

Firmness and discipline are necessary, yes—but always tempered with the love, forgiveness, and mercy that God continually extends to us. There is an old saying, "God's gifts to you can be blocked by the refusal to pass them on to others."

God has favored most Americans with housing and food far beyond the reach of all but the very rich in other countries and in former centuries. Most of mankind over the ages has lived in hovels and eaten food that would appall us. The income of the average United States wage earner today is the envy of the workers in nearly every other country.

What has this to do with business ethics? Well, just go back to the days when mining operations were in isolated areas, far away from any towns. Company-owned stores were set up, and miners' families had to buy their food and clothing there because there were no other stores. In those days the temptation was great for some companies to charge unconscionable prices for their goods. This practice denied to the miners all but a subsistence living level.

A comparable situation today would be a slumlord—the owner of an apartment in the inner city who does not maintain his property. The rent is as high as he can get, and yet he does not replace a faltering and dangerous furnace or repair a leaking roof. He takes the tenants' money but puts back as little as possible into maintenance and service.

The overpricing of goods and services neglects this ethic of gratitude for what God has already abundantly given. There are moral as well as economic consequences to many business decisions.

Our high standard of living has also accorded us longer lives and singularly improved health services. Imagine, if you can, what an operation or an amputation would have been like without the blessing of anesthesia. Even something as undramatic as a simple headache must have temporarily devastated people before the discovery of aspirin! We are indeed fortunate to be living today.

Following the same line of ethical reasoning, most manufacturers of everything from toys and machines to drugs and food products will not knowingly release any item that jeopardizes the safety or health of a user. In appreciation for their own good health, even an economic loss is preferable to risking the lives of others.

Now I happen to believe that American business is ethically managed. I don't believe that the occasional newspaper story of some sensationally corrupt executive reflects accurately life in America or in American business. Corruption is and always has been a part of our world. So have inefficiency, laziness, and sloppy bookkeeping. But I do not share the cynical disillusionment of those who might say, "Ethical behavior is a good idea, but only for those that I'm dealing with." Top executives, in my experience, are very bright men and women. They know, along with industrial psychologists, that the best fuel to drive any organization is a strong moral commitment by the chief executive officer.

In his pedantic book, *The Functions of the Executive*, Chester I. Barnard describes this sort of commitment as "the aspect of leadership we commonly imply in the word *responsibility*, the quality which gives dependability and determination to human conduct, and foresight and ideality to purpose."

Barnard later continues, "Without leadership in this supreme sense, the inherent difficulties often cannot be overcome even for short periods."

Terrence E. Deal and Allen A. Kennedy also discuss the economic importance of moral values. They say in *Corporate Cultures: The Rites and Rituals of Corporate Life* that the values of a business, which they term its culture, can make or break corporate strategy. They add that it is the leader who gives that culture its quality.

A national bestseller is Thomas J. Peters and Robert H. Waterman, Jr.'s book, *In Search of Excellence*. In a discussion of organizational values they say with admirable insight, "Values are clear; they are acted out minute by minute and decade by decade by the top brass; and they are well understood deep in the companies' ranks."

Business ethics courses, interestingly enough, have proliferated in our colleges. A Bentley College survey in 1982 found three hundred seventeen schools with business-ethics classes, about five times as many as in 1973.

Smart people realize that ethical sensitivity is not just good for the soul; it is also extremely good business. We all like to deal with an ethical salesman or an ethical firm. Trust builds sales volume. It gives that individual or that company a decided edge over competitors.

Okay. Assuming you agree on the desirability of a first-rate ethical code, how do you go about constructing one? There are four steps you might consider:

1. Resolve that the time taken to do this is worthwhile and will be beneficial to you. The Harvard psychologist, A. M. Nicholi, Jr. has said, "The first aspect of a healthy mind comprises a sound, consistent conscience with well defined moral precepts."

2. Has your interest or curiosity been aroused by the mentioning of biblical ethics? If so, in addition to Leviticus and Deuteronomy, especially reread the book of Proverbs. Write down God's instructions that you feel could apply to your life in today's world. Then, read from the New Testament, particularly Jesus' Sermon on the Mount in Matthew 5, 6, and 7. List his important directives. Do you see any modifications of what you wrote down previously?

3. Ronald C. Wade, a managing partner in the accounting firm of Arthur Anderson & Co., gives a helpful tip. He says he sometimes inserts his own name when he comes across an ethical statement in the Bible. For example, he reads Proverbs 24:17 as, "Do not rejoice, Ron, when your enemy falls, and let not your heart be glad when he stumbles." This personalizes the imperative of the passage and brings the point of it home to him in a forceful way. You might try this as you formulate your own code.

4. Now you are ready to put all of this in some order. One suggestion is that your code have two parts—one, a list of those things you will do, and two, a list of things you will not do.

In the first tabulation, put such statements as, "I will handle each customer's account with professional competence and imagination, considering his interests as though I were in his place" (The Golden Rule).

Or if you are in management, you might have something like, "I will place my personal integrity and that of my people ahead of my keen desire to increase profits" (Mark 8:36 KJV: "For what shall it profit a man, if he shall gain the whole world, and lose his own soul?").

The second list will contain statements of what you will *not* do: "I will not lie; I will not cheat," et cetera (the Ten Commandments sort of prohibitions). Then consider your particular situation. In my case, I have had a long-standing rule concerning customers that I neither like nor respect. If I believe them to be honest, I'll certainly do business with them, and I'll even entertain them if necessary. But, I will not invite them into my home to meet my wife.

I did break this rule one time in what was truly a case of desperation. I had not been married very long when the head of our firm called me to his office. He told me that a most important client from a distant city would be in town that night. It seemed that none of our senior executives was available to have dinner with this man who controlled a large account. So he assigned me to the task.

Right after work, I proudly picked this man up at his hotel and took him to one of the city's best restaurants. We passed a delightful couple of hours, and I was congratulating myself on doing a great job for the firm when without warning, he asked a blunt question that caused my bubble to collapse. As he lit up an after-dinner cigar, he looked hard at me and said, "When do we get the girls?"

For a moment I was speechless as I tried to think fast. This was totally unexpected, and I decided to be candid about that. I told him that the thought had not entered my mind. I confessed that I had not the foggiest notion of where to obtain a call girl or prostitute for him. But realizing that my response could lose this account, I came up with what turned out to be a darn good solution.

During dinner he had mentioned that he liked to sing. Luckily, I had remembered that. Quickly I said, "Mr. Blank, you said you liked to sing. Well, I have a little bride at home who is a musician. She can play the piano by ear so well I'll bet you can't think of a song she can't play."

"Let's go see," he said and off we went.

I alerted my wife, and when we arrived there was more food and drink awaiting us. She played, and we three sang for what seemed like hours. He had a rotten voice, but he thoroughly enjoyed himself. So much so, in fact, that on future trips to our city, he never again mentioned girls but only coming to my house to sing. Fortunately, I have a wife who not only will put up with that sort of inconvenience, but she actually enters into it with enthusiasm. I went against one of my ethical rules, it is true, but I think it probably was the right thing to do.

Now that you have written out your personal code of ethics, you are in an enviable position. If you will set these rules of conduct so firmly in your mind that they even extend down into the subconscious, then you really do have an advantage over many others. Let me explain.

More than ten years ago, my executive vice president gave

me an eloquently written statement on ethics and morality. It was on a plain sheet of bond paper with no clues as to who had written it. He had discovered it among some old papers. Since then I have tried to locate its source. Even reference librarians, those persistent souls, have been unable to track it down. Here it is, slightly shortened. If you know who wrote it, I would certainly like to have that information.

"Anyone . . . who has strong convictions about the rights and wrongs of . . . morality, has a very great advantage in times of strain, since his instincts on what to do are clear and immediate. Lacking such a framework or moral conviction of what is right and what is wrong, he is forced to lean almost entirely upon his mental possessions; he adds up the pluses and minuses of any question and comes up with a conclusion. Under normal conditions, when he is not tired or frustrated, this pragmatic approach should successfully bring him out on the right side of the question. What worries me are the conclusions that such an individual may reach when he is tired, angry, frustrated, or emotionally affected."

That statement is about the best summation I can imagine on the value of a code of ethics.

Sports writers have often referred to Tom Watson as the greatest golfer in the world. He has won nearly every major golf tournament at least once and many of them several times. Fame and fortune have not spoiled him. He is respected as well as admired by all who have followed his outstanding career.

Both his skill and integrity were evident at an early age. He had his heart set on becoming a champion. He also had his personal code of honor firmly in mind. In the first state tournament that he ever entered, he put his putter down behind his ball on one of the greens. To his dismay, the ball moved slightly. No one saw it. Of that he was certain. He was under great pressure to win, and there was no time whatever to add up the pluses and minuses of the alternatives. But he knew without hesitation what he must do; he went over to an official and said, "My ball moved." That action cost him a stroke, and he lost the hole. Tom Watson placed his personal integrity ahead of his keen desire to win.

Happily, as it turned out, he did succeed in winning the match. He came back to win that particular state tournament three more times. He has gone on to win world championships, fame, international renown, and lives a truly happy life with an unblemished conscience.

As Jesus so truly promised, "But seek first [God's] kingdom and his righteousness, and all these things shall be yours as well" (Matthew 6:33).

Chapter Six

POSITIVE THINKING WITH A TWIST
Patience and the Smorgasbord Theory

What would you say is the single most important factor for success in business? Would you point to intelligence as the vital ingredient? Is it business school training that propels some to the top? Or is it chiefly a matter of just plain luck?

It is pretty obvious that it would be helpful to anyone to have them all—high intelligence, excellent training, and good luck. And, of course, I would add that a personal code of ethical behavior is particularly necessary for the overall kind of success we've been talking about.

But it takes more than any of the foregoing to forge ahead in a business or profession. Many writers have pointed out that *the* critical determinant in what people do with their lives is attitude. One of the most notable of these writers is Norman Vincent Peale, whose book *The Power of Positive Thinking* made publishing history. If you're ambitious and haven't read it, that's a mistake (sin)!

It's not my intention to propose any formula, magic or otherwise, for developing positive thinking. I'm often suspicious of pat prescriptions, anyway. I remember reading of a California man who was interviewed when he was one hundred and three years old. Some of his rules for a long life were:

> *Smoke eight $1.35 cigars a day.*
> *Drink wine with every meal.*

Three or four scotch and sodas daily.
Skip sex for a whole year once every ten years.

According to the report, he refused to say whether or not this was a rest year in the cycle!

Rather than rules, I'd like to discuss two ideas that can lead you to develop a winning attitude:

Positive Patience

The Smorgasbord Theory

Positive Patience

In the Navy the officer on the bridge who directs the progress of a ship is said to have the "conn." This word comes from *conduen* (Middle English), which means "to conduct"—one who directs or leads. In a business, someone or some group must be generating forward thinking and strategic planning if that business is to progress and prosper. It is true that planned goals are often missed, but would you knowingly go to work for a firm whose announced philosophy was, "We don't aim at nothin', so we can't hardly miss"?

The same holds true for your life. Your thoughts are the pilot of your life. They have the conn as to which direction you will go in business and in life, forward or backward, up or down. If there are only rambling thoughts, then you have lost steering control, and like a ship you'll either drift aimlessly or else be "dead in the water," going nowhere. Many a person has stayed in the same dull job until retirement. Undisturbed water, we know, often turns stagnant.

But, there *is* such a thing as *positive patience*. Few can say that they have made steady progress without interruptions.

Waiting can be productive if accepted with self-control and courage. It is that combination that I call positive patience.

Let me tell you the story of Joseph, the lad who legend says wore a coat of many colors. Oh, sure—we all remember that old Bible story, but have you thought of it in this light, that positive patience can lead to the very height of worldly power and success?

Joseph was a brash youth, having at first neither humility nor psychological insight. He incensed his half-brothers by his boasting that someday they would all bow down to him. Finally in a jealous rage, they first threw him into the wilderness pit to die, then, changing their minds, they sold him into slavery in Egypt. He was bought by one of Pharaoh's officers to whom he proved himself reliable. He was soon put in charge of all that belonged to his master. Presently, trouble again struck. Refusing the advances of his master's wife, he was falsely accused by her. He was thrown into prison for more than two years during which he won the confidence and even the friendship of the jailer and his fellow prisoners by interpreting their dreams.

Then the Pharaoh dreamed a dream that no one could interpret. Joseph was remembered and sent for. He accurately analyzed the dream, predicting that there would be seven years of great plenty throughout the land to be followed by seven years of failure. He advised the king to store the produce of the seven good years, and Pharaoh placed him in full charge.

There is much more to the story—how he prospered and how he was united with his father and brothers, but it's Joseph's attitude of positive patience that is the point here. In all of his dire predicaments he never gave way to panic. In the wilderness pit, as a slave in Egypt, or in prison, he maintained his self-control and his courage. Just as importantly, he threw himself energetically into his work even while waiting in prison. Others might sulk or rebel or even give up and die. But Joseph's nature was to do his best, while patiently waiting for things to improve.

Joseph was a man whose faith in God gave him the strength under duress to discipline his thoughts and thus achieve positive patience. That faith and patience led him to the highest post he could occupy in an alien land.

But, make no mistake, Joseph had the other necessary attributes as well. It is obvious from the story that he was no dummy. God had given him a sharp mind. Under his Egyptian master he also had excellent training in administration. I can't imagine that he was not a hard worker. He undoubtedly was willing to put in long hours learning his skills and would never have expressed the discouragement of Chaucer's narrator, "The lyf so short, the craft so long to lerne, Th'assay so hard. . . ." Put all of his attributes together with controlled patience, and he was bound to have good luck.

Joseph lived nearly four thousand years ago, and no one is sure just how historical every part of the Joseph story is. But here's a story of just forty years ago that is completely factual.

Dr. James Lally grew up in a suburb of Chicago—Blue Island, Illinois. His father was a surgeon, and that is exactly what Jim dreamed about and longed to become.

The glorious day finally arrived when he was admitted to medical school—Northwestern University, no less. You can imagine how his thoughts raced with elation.

Once a year, all medical students were given routine physical exams. At the beginning of Jim's final year at Northwestern his world suddenly fell apart. The medical dean called him into his office and told him he had tuberculosis.

There were no drugs with which to treat T.B. at that time—nothing like streptomycin or rifampin that we have today. There was no way to predict whether or not a patient would even recover. The only treatment was to stay in bed for an entire year.

Imagine the shock to be within two semesters of becoming an M.D. and to be cruelly yanked out of the school and perhaps out of a career.

Riding home that day on the rattling, dirty commuter train was the absolute low point of his life. All his dreams were vanishing. He did not know whether he would live or die. And he was so full of life! He was a superior boxer, active in the Catholic Youth Organization and the Golden Gloves. That summer he had taken flying lessons early each morning, then hurried into Chicago to work all day in a medical laboratory which he loved. After work he attended school each evening before reaching home again.

Now all this activity was over. His body would become flabby, his muscles lose their tone as he lay month after month in bed. Those first few weeks were difficult, especially when his medical school friends would stop by to tell him what they were doing and learning. He was sunk in despair.

Then his mother sat herself down and gave him some straight talk. She knew how to reach him with her gentle yet pointed discourse—urging courage instead of despondency; self-control, not self-pity. Jim began to utilize positive patience. It's marvelous how a good mother can bring her child around!

He perked up and commenced a thoughtfully planned reading program, which he followed for the entire year. He read medical books, medical journals, and for a change of pace, he read every word that Shakespeare ever wrote!

Like Joseph, the ending of this story is also a positive experience. He reentered medical school a year later, weak and out of condition. But due to his year of reading he was well prepared for his courses, so he found the time to exercise and reform his body. He had learned to concentrate and to enjoy extensive reading. This further eased his way in the last year of school and has stuck with him ever since. He was delayed a year, no doubt of that, but he had learned to think positively. His subsequent success as a general surgeon, husband, father, and church leader attests to the value of that year of positive patience. Without it he could have easily fallen prey to negative thinking.

I once knew a young contractor who was rapidly rising in the construction business. I used to have lunch with him once or twice a year. We met one noon, and I was shocked at his appearance. He looked years older, and I noticed his hands trembling as he reached for a glass of water.

"Have you been sick, Joe?" I inquired.

"No," he replied, "but I well may be before the end of another month."

He explained that he had bid on a huge job, larger than anything he had ever done before. He was confident he could complete it successfully—that wasn't a concern. The problem was the terrible suspense of not knowing for at least a month whether or not his bid would be the winning one. Because there was a great deal of money in it for him, he could not control his thoughts. The month of waiting was literally killing him.

The postscript to this story is that he did *not* get the job. I don't know how that news affected him, but later when we were again together, he was back to normal in health and appearance. I might add that neither of us ever again brought up the subject of that one long, painful month of impatient waiting and its negative influence on his health.

The Smorgasbord Theory

There is a theory that I believe you'll find useful in directing your thinking into positive channels. I call it the Smorgasbord Theory. The idea behind this theory is not mine, but I have never seen it expressed in this connection or called by any such name.

What in the world is the Smorgasbord Theory—and how is it useful? To respond first to the second part of the question, Wally Amos, the originator of "Famous Amos" chocolate chip cookies, once made a thought-provoking statement in an interview. He said, "Most of us have great ideas. But we bury them inside us, under the debris of self-doubt and resentment and spite. You are limitless when you let go of the rubbish." The Smorgasbord Theory points the way to a release of all such negative thoughts.

Its thesis is that God is the creator of all life and all things that are in existence. Moreover, he must also have originated every personality trait that we humans possess. To say otherwise would mean that we mere mortals have certain characteristics that God, himself, does not have. Where would they have come from? We cannot produce anything from nothing. Consequently, our emotions cannot be unknown to God; they must also exist in him.

This idea, of course, goes back to the fourth century B.C., to Plato who lived in Athens. His view was that all the realities of this world, whether they be material objects or mental images and concepts, are restricted as to time and space. All such worldly realities, however, have an ideal form in the eternal world, which is free from all of their limitations. Our world and all it contains is merely an imitation or copy of the ultimate world of ideal forms.

Now back to the Smorgasbord Theory—it affirms that we are created in God's image. If you accept that statement at face value, then it follows that God logically could be assumed to have all of our traits. And perhaps he does not have only ones like love, kindness, mercy, and compassion.

The early books of the Old Testament indicate the people thought of Jehovah as very much like themselves. That is to say that they often thought of him as a warlike God, a God of vengeance (Jeremiah 50:15), jealousy (Exodus 20:5), capable of hatred (Amos 5:21; 6:8) and anger (Numbers 11:16).

He could be a punishing deity, sometimes pitiless (Jeremiah 20:16), filled with fierce rage (II Chronicles 28:11). At times they viewed him as deceitful (Jeremiah 20:7) and even capable of planning evil (Exodus 32:14; I Chronicles 21:15).

Taking all of this into consideration, the theory maintains that God contains all human traits just as a smorgasbord table a block long could have on it every food known to man.

Suppose you have a large plate and are walking the length of that great table. You are free to select any of the hundreds of foods arrayed there. You could wisely choose the healthful, nourishing items. You could also, with some effort, pick out only the sour things such as pickles, lemons, persimmons, vinegar, and, to my taste at least, sauerkraut. Why anyone would want to fill a plate with such acerbity I can't imagine. If persisted in, that diet would soon corrode even the staunchest stomach!

Yet this is just what some of us are doing every day in our relationship with God. If we think he is a stern, bitter, punishing God—well, he does have those qualities. They are there in him just as the persimmons are there on the buffet table. If that is all that we find in God, so the theory goes, then that is all that we will receive from him. This block-long table with all its food and our God who encompasses all characteristics have far more choices than any one of us can appropriate. So, we have to decide just what we are going to choose.

The wonderful thing about this theory is that we can choose to believe that God is very personally concerned with our making a success of our particular life. We can elect to ask God for his loving care, protection, and assistance—things that will bring us to the best possible solution for every problem we face. And we can ask this from him with the same expectation of receiving it as if we were asking a waitress behind the buffet table to give us a serving of fruit.

We can rely on the Bible for that assurance. Mark 11:23 and 24 say exactly that, but with two qualifications. In these verses, Jesus says that if you have the same degree of faith in God as you have that a waitress will serve you, and if you have forgiven any and all who have offended you, then what you ask for in prayer will be given to you. But be sure to heed the warning of the old stoic philosopher, Seneca, who said, "Don't pray for what you'll wish you hadn't gotten."

Sometimes it happens that what you order in a restaurant isn't ready yet. It still has to be prepared for you. If you are hungry for a magnificent roast beef, you might have to wait several hours before you could eat it. If you "raised Cain" in that restaurant and demanded that it be brought to you instantly, the poor chef could only bring out a raw and inedible mass.

Similarly, positive patience is also required with our prayers of faith. We must believe not only that God will solve our problems and give us what we hunger for, but that he also knows far better than we what the timing should be for his answers to our prayers. They will come when all is in readiness. "They who wait for the Lord shall renew their strength; they shall mount up with wings like eagles, they shall run and not be weary, they shall walk and not faint" (Isaiah 40:31).

In very large measure our attitude steers the voyage of our lives. The odds for success are the most favorable when we firmly believe that God is to us exactly as we expect him to be. We then trust that he will give us good gifts. He will do it at once or later as he knows best.

Years ago, a sales manager sent a young inexperienced trainee out to make cold canvass calls. Those are sales calls where the salesman does not know the prospect. He just drops in cold, so to speak. That is the toughest kind of sale to make, and usually there's a good deal of fear and trepidation involved in working up the nerve to enter the prospect's office.

When the youngster returned that afternoon with two nice orders, the manager was frankly surprised at such a good result.

"How did you manage to do it?" he asked.

"Well," the young salesman replied, "before I started out I knew I needed a winning attitude. So I said a brief prayer. I reminded God that I could be rather easily discouraged. I asked him to give me some success today, as a test, to see if I am really meant to sell insurance. I asked that he suspend the law of averages, just for now—and then when I've had more experience and can better take the turn-downs that come to all salesmen—then let that law work a little overtime and catch up! I was not requesting any long-term favors."

He continued, "I believed that God would do that for me, and he did! Now, I'm so excited I want to spend the next thirty years of my life selling insurance."

And indeed that is exactly what he did do—because, you see—I was that young salesman.

Chapter Seven

THE FEARFUL TRAP
How to Avoid Fear

Lead on, O King eternal, We follow, not with fears . . .
                                        Henry Smart

One of Franklin D. Roosevelt's most memorable statements was his Great Depression speech in which he told the
American people, "The only thing we have to fear is fear
itself." Even those who are too young to remember him are
familiar with those words just as they recognize the "blood,
. . . tears, and sweat" quotation from Winston Churchill.

Instinctively, we seem to know that fear is our enemy; yet
we still fall often into its trap. Our hearts and nerves fail us
and, yet, as Amelia Earhart Putnam once said, "Courage is
the price that life exacts for granting peace." Perhaps
Thoreau was thinking of fear when he wrote, "The mass of
men lead lives of quiet desperation."

It has struck me that the more successful people are in
whatever they are doing, the higher degree of supremacy they
have usually won over fear. Some psychologists now think
that when we fear it is because whatever we most trust is not
big enough or strong enough to sustain us. We tend to believe
in something with primary value for us. If it is something that
can fail us, then subconsciously, at least, we worry and are
unsure and afraid. It may be that we put our trust in monetary
wealth and become anxious as we watch it wax and wane. We
may lean on fame or personal power or pleasure, but these are
weak reeds indeed, and in our hearts we know it.

It may be that our trust is in ourselves, in our own abilities and in our superior brain, but we are not strong enough to meet all that life may hold. To believe solely in our own capabilities is to open wide the door to anxiety and fear. Also, to believe that this is not an intelligently managed universe is to feel lonely and insecure.

People often go to great lengths to protect themselves from the thing they fear most. An insurance friend of mine on the East Coast told me this extreme example. He once insured the home of a man who lived in dread of fire. The man was so fearful of being trapped by fire that he employed the best fire prevention engineers to design for him an absolutely fireproof house. Now, most insurance people will tell you there really is no way to build a truly fireproof dwelling. The best you can do is build one that is fire-resistant.

This man, nevertheless, was determined to have a fireproof house, and he may have come closer to it than anyone else ever has. Everything in that house was made of nonflammable materials. The rugs, the drapes, the upholstery were all of synthetic materials that would not burn. Some of the very clothes that he had his family wear were sprayed to make them fire-resistant.

Great care was exercised in the way electricity and gas were introduced into the house. But in the unlikely event that fire somehow did occur in an appliance, the house was complete with automatic sprinklers and fireproof doors. He even held periodic drills for his family and servants so that it became second nature to close those doors whenever they left any area of the home.

This man put his trust in that house. He believed it to be secure from fire and, obviously, that was of primary importance to him. I don't imagine it was the most comfortable place to live in, but then, that was not his priority.

One day when the family was away, the houseman was doing some ironing in the basement. The doorbell rang. He hurried upstairs, neglecting to turn off the iron, but from habit, he did close the fireproof door to the basement. At the front door he read a telegram informing him of the death of a loved one. Hurriedly, he packed some clothes and took off.

In the meantime, the iron grew hot and a small fire broke out. The owner knew that something like that might happen, and before long one of the sprinklers opened and put out the blaze. It then shut off, as it was supposed to do.

What could not have been foreseen was that the fire chanced to be directly beneath a joint or connection in the gas line. Before the sprinkler head operated there was time for the heat of the flame to melt the sealing of that pipe. After the fire was out, gas continued to leak from the pipe until eventually the nearly airtight basement was full of gas. All it took then was a spark from the furnace starting up to have the biggest, most devastating explosion you can imagine!

My insurance friend said the house was literally blown apart. There weren't many pieces left bigger than a wheelbarrow. They just shoveled it away. In spite of, or maybe because of, all his fearful planning, that little fire totally destroyed the house that was built to be fireproof. What he trusted in was not strong enough to sustain him.

When I was a boy I must have displayed some timidity. Evidently, I had more fear than my father thought I should. He had me memorize a little poem intended to correct that particular flaw in my make-up. By now I have forgotten all but the last line, which has stuck with me ever since.

The poem, as I remember it, is about a nervous, shrinking fellow who decides he will not go out with the hunters that day because he hears a lion roaring in the forest—he is afraid to go out with the sailors because the sea is rough. So he stays at home, thinking himself secure in the well-protected city. That evening the hunters returned safely from the woods, the sailors safe from the sea, but "The city that was founded upon a rock was swallowed up by an earthquake shock."

There are few absolutes in life. Certain it is that there are no surefire ways to protect ourselves from every manner of frightful thing that can befall human beings. And, indeed, some degree of fear is a necessity. Can you picture a totally fearless person? I doubt that a person who threw caution to the wind and dashed heedlessly about could survive long.

What kind of fear then should we have? The Lord spoke to the old prophet, Isaiah, and told him not to be afraid of *any* of the things that other people feared. Isaiah was to fear God instead, and then, the promise was, that he wouldn't need to be afraid of anything else. That's quite a promise! If we actually do fear God, meaning to love and trust him, then we'll never know the unhealthy fears that produce stress, anxiety, and panic. King David in the thirty-fourth psalm affirms, "I sought the Lord, and he . . . delivered me from all my fears." God *is* big enough for our trust.

The ninety-first psalm makes what appears to be some outlandish promises—promises such as safety, honor, long life, and salvation. No matter what happens to all about you, this psalm promises that it need not come near you. It is a lovely affirmation of what God earnestly intends for every life.

I suspect that too many read this psalm supposing that it is really nothing but powerful poetic imagery. After all, worldly common sense scoffs at such seemingly unredeemable pledges.

Upon a closer reading of this psalm, however, you will find three conditions that must be met before the psalmist's declarations can take effect. The three conditions are *prayer*, *trust*, and *fearlessness*.

"He who dwells in the shelter of the Most High,
   who abides in the shadow of the Almighty,
will say to the LORD, 'My refuge and my fortress;
   my God, in whom I trust.'
For he will deliver you from the snare of the fowler
   and from the deadly pestilence;
he will cover you with his pinions,
and under his wings you will find refuge;
   his faithfulness is a shield and buckler.
You will not fear the terror of the night,
   nor the arrow that flies by day,
nor the pestilence that stalks in darkness,
   nor the destruction that wastes at noonday.

A thousand may fall at your side,
   ten thousand at your right hand;
   but it will not come near you.
You will only look with your eyes
   and see the recompense of the wicked.

Because you have made the LORD your refuge,
   the Most High your habitation,
no evil shall befall you,
   no scourge come near your tent.

For he will give his angels charge of you
   to guard you in all your ways.
On their hands they will bear you up,
   lest you dash your foot against a stone.
You will tread on the lion and the adder,
   the young lion and the serpent you will trample under foot.

Because he cleaves to me in love, I will deliver him;
   I will protect him, because he knows my name.

When he calls to me, I will answer him;
   I will be with him in trouble,
   I will rescue him and honor him.
With long life I will satisfy him,
   and show him my salvation " (Psalm 91).

It is easy to pick out the reference to frequent prayer and meditation. We are told to dwell and abide in his shelter, to cleave to him in love, and to make him our refuge and habitation. This psalm states that regular and heartfelt prayer is the condition for its promise of safety. It is not enough to run for God's shelter only when trouble or danger threatens. We are to keep in regular contact with him.

The second stipulation that should be noticed in the psalm is that of trust. God's protection is for those who can honestly say, "My refuge and my fortress; my God, in whom I trust." There must not be the slightest element of doubt—only complete trust that God will deliver as he has promised. Can you make that ringing declaration?

The final requisite is an outgrowth of the first two: we are now to have no fear. No matter what is taking place in the world around us. This psalm says you will not fear. We are to go on living our lives confidently and unafraid. As we do so, God promises to use his unlimited, mighty power to keep us from all harm.

If the promises of this psalm still seem preposterous to you, keep in mind that the three conditions are tough ones to satisfy. There is nothing easy about all of this, and that is why such guarantees may seem unrealistic. But the three conditions *can* be met. With patience, prayer, and practice, they can be accomplished.

Daily routines may need to be rearranged to give more time for prayer, but with careful planning that can be done.

It is more difficult to achieve complete trust and lack of fear. It takes time and the realization that sheer courage is not the answer. Mark Twain once said in a serious vein, "Courage is resistance to fear, mastery of fear, not absence of fear." So, if not by courage, how then can fear be eliminated and trust substituted for it?

The *love* of God can and will eliminate fear and lead to total trust. In the book of I John is this statement, "There is no fear in love, but perfect love casts out fear" (4:18). Consequently, we can say that where there is perfect love for God, there can be no fear; where there is fear, it simply means that there is not as yet perfect love. There is a phrase to remember. When we doubt God's ability to solve a problem, our trust begins to erode into apprehension and fear. That is the time to bolster up the love of God and to reaffirm that with perfect love, there can be no fears or doubts.

Here is how one woman handled her fear of flying. Lisa Johnson is an attractive, middle-aged woman who is married to a successful man. Because his work entails travel to other countries, he has always liked to take his wife along on some of his trips, and he can afford to do so.

There used to be a problem, however. Lisa was terrified of flying. Whenever she did have to fly, she fortified herself with several drinks before boarding the plane, and she would continue drinking on the plane until she was nearly senseless. She was no companion for her husband on the flight, and the next day, she was usually sick from so much alcohol. This routine was, of course, repeated on the way home. Lisa was invited less and less to accompany him, and she was actually in some danger of becoming an alcoholic.

Then Lisa discovered an overlooked verse in the Bible. I quote here from the King James version because I think that version aims more directly at the individual reading it.

Isaiah 41:10 is one of God's most powerful promises to all the fearful who call upon God to protect them. It reads, "Fear thou not; for I am with thee: be not dismayed; for I am thy God: I will strengthen thee; yea, I will help thee; yea, I will uphold thee with the right hand of my righteousness."

Lisa Johnson saw the light, as this verse came alive for her. She said it over and over as she took her seat on the airplane. She inserted her own name in it, whispering to herself, "Fear thou not, Lisa, for I am with thee. . . ." Soon she began believing what she was saying and trusting in it. That part about God upholding her with his right hand seemed directed point-blank at her fear of flying. Now she goes with her husband anytime without fear and without alcohol. Yes, she saw the light, and as the English writer John Ruskin said, "To see clearly is poetry, prophecy, and religion, all in one."

One of the most often repeated admonitions throughout the Bible is "Fear thou not." We can overcome fear because as one proverb puts it, "The fear of man lays a snare, but he who trusts in the Lord is safe" (29:25).

Without fear, life in a home or in an office is smoother and work more pleasant. Everyone in their heart desires such peace. They struggle to achieve it in different ways—some by expensive counseling sessions and others by reading the assurances of the Bible, and believing them and growing into perfect love for God, which casts out all fear.

We long to understand our environment and to make it conform to our needs. Elusive as such a consonance may be for many, those who live by God's promises find that Herman Melville, the author of *Moby Dick*, was right when he wrote, "For as this appalling ocean surrounds the verdant land, so in the soul of man there lies one insular Tahiti, full of peace and joy [though] encompassed by all the horrors of the half-known life."

Chapter Eight

GOD DON'T MAKE NO TRASH
Developing a Positive Self-Image

Whoever first spoke those words—"God don't make no trash"—was giving forth some good old-fashioned common sense. Every soul is the work of the master craftsman. As such, it deserves to be treated with esteem.

Almost everyone would agree with that last statement in principle; yet a great many people believe themselves to be inferior to others and actually hold themselves in low esteem. Psychiatrists often report that depression is the most common ailment they treat. People severely depressed see both life and themselves as virtually worthless.

How do you view yourself? In your own mind are you trash, or are you a child of God? Some folks, I guess, even imagine themselves to be some sort of gods. Possibly they might appear to be that to others, although not usually to those who know them best!

In this connection, William A. Hall, assistant to the chairman of Hallmark Cards and president of the Hall Family Foundations, tells a cute story regarding his young son. Bill Hall and his son were driving in the car the day after the "tooth fairy" had left a coin beneath the little fellow's pillow. In a pensive mood he looked over at his father and asked, "Daddy, are you really the tooth fairy?"

His father, deciding the time had come to stop the pretending, said, "Yes, son, I am."

After a few thoughtful minutes came the next question, "Daddy, are you also Santa Claus?"

"Well, yes, son, I am."

"Then, Daddy, is Mommy God?"

How do you view yourself—as someone special or as trash? Would you agree with the cynical view of certain modern philosophers? For example, the English Nobel prize winner, Bertrand Russell, believed that man is but a helpless atom.

Lord Byron wrote, "O man! thou feeble tenant of an hour / Debased by slavery, or corrupt by power, / Who knows thee well must quit thee with disgust, / Degraded mass of animated dust!"

Let's hope you firmly reject all such pessimism and despair. It is especially important in business or a profession to have a positive self-image. Those with a defeatist attitude inspire no confidence in others. People somehow are able to sense how a person views himself. If you think you are trash, don't be too surprised if others agree with you!

For a positive and quite marvelous expression concerning all humans, you can go all the way back to the first century after Christ. The Jewish rabbi Akiba wrote with true insight, "Beloved is man, for he was created in the image of God; but it was by a special love that it was made known to him that he was created in the image of God."

That's really a wonderful statement. Now, how do we know for sure that we are made in the likeness of God? Well, the first chapter of Genesis, our manual, proclaims that man is indeed created in the likeness of God. Then in the second chapter of Paul's letter to the Hebrews there is the triumphant assertion that we are made only "a little lower than the angels" (Heb. 2:7 KJV).

I like that definition of man a great deal better than those dismal ones of the cynics, don't you? The simple eloquence of that phrase "a little lower than the angels" should be uplifting to any downcast spirit. We are not helpless atoms, idiots, or sick flies. Divinity itself was the blueprint from which we were fashioned—and that cannot be trash.

When we make something, carefully following a blueprint, it is only logical to suppose that we have a worthwhile purpose for it. We have a plan in our minds for its use; otherwise, why would we go to the trouble of making it?

So it is with God. Isn't it reasonable to assume that he has a plan in his mind for every life that he brings forth? The master reference book confirms that assumption. It is full of encouraging information. Take the book of Proverbs. I like Proverbs because the verses are short and snappy. They get right to the point without extraneous detail. The sixteenth chapter of that book comes right out squarely:

> "Commit your work to the LORD,
>   and your plans will be established.
> The LORD has made everything for its purpose"
>   (Prov. 16:3-4a).

According to Proverbs, we should ask God to show us the plans he has for our lives.

> "Trust in the LORD with all your heart,
>   and do not rely on your own insight.
> In all your ways acknowledge him,
>   and he will make straight your paths" (3:5-6).

It is also true that we have the power of self-determination. But if we rely solely upon ourselves, not attempting to discover God's plan for our lives, might not that be a root

95

cause for much of our stress and unhappiness? There is some straight talk in Proverbs:

"He who trusts in his own mind is a fool" (28:26*a*).

The psalmist has similar thoughts:

"thou dost hold my right hand.
Thou dost guide me with thy counsel" (73:23*b*-24*a*).

Isaiah sums it all up beautifully:

"And I will lead the blind
in a way that they know not,
in paths that they have not known
I will guide them.
I will turn the darkness before them into light,
the rough places into level ground.
These are the things I will do,
and I will not forsake them" (42:16).

In a very real sense, we are all blind. We cannot see one day, one hour, or even one minute ahead of us down life's pathway. It's that fact that can give rise to feelings of fear and helplessness. Did you ever ride on the observation platform of an old-style Pullman train? The last car of the train often had an open deck at the rear with a railing around it and three or four chairs on it. You could sit there looking back along the track and the countryside through which you had just passed, listening to the rhythmical clicking of the wheels. But you could not see one mile, one yard, or even one foot ahead on the train's pathway. You simply had to trust that the track was all laid out before you and that it led to your destination.

Our lives are very much like that. The odds are that we will be the most free of anxiety, fear and, yes, even depression when we trust that God has laid out the track ahead of us with a fulfilling destination in mind.

It is an exhilarating thought. We can't be trash if God himself is offering to guide us through life. That's having a little slice of heaven right here on earth. As Jesus once said to one who answered him wisely, "You are not far from the kingdom of God" (Mark 12:34).

The wisdom that is needed for a life free from trashy self-doubts can be acquired in several ways. Here are two of them: The first has to do with experience which, of course, is the basis of much of our learning. We learn not only from what we're taught, but also from what happens to us. Wisdom often comes by benefitting from our mistakes. Here's an amusing story about a close friend in Boston whose name I won't mention because I want to keep his friendship!

This man is intellectual, capable, and before he retired, he was the head of a prominent company. Some years ago he was bothered by a toothache. This puzzled him because he had always brushed his teeth regularly. Upon visiting his dentist he was genuinely surprised to learn that people are supposed to brush on the *inside* as well as the outside of their teeth. He had been religiously cleaning only the front! That one toothache put him on the right track and saved him from more misery later on.

In a similar way we can be grateful for experiencing other small warnings that, if we're wise enough to heed promptly, may very well save us from jumping the track that God has laid out for us. They can serve to prod us in the right direction.

During World War II, I was assigned to help put a destroyer into commission on Staten Island in New York Harbor. During that time I often took the ferry back and forth to Manhattan. I always liked to be up forward on the bow as we docked. I would watch with admiration the skill of the captain as he maneuvered the ferryboat at just the correct angle to counteract the forces of the tide and wind. But even with all the pilot's expertise there still needed to be a row of pilings on either side of the slip to shunt the boat gently back to its proper heading whenever it was off course and veering toward trouble.

It is easy for us to tell when we are off our proper course. That's when fears and anxieties begin to creep in—moderately at first, gently nudging us like the pilings nudge a ship, back to God's plan for our lives. When we respond to those early warnings, the odds increase in favor of our avoiding far more serious consequences such as depression. This type of wisdom is crammed into all the thirty-one chapters of Proverbs.

There is a second way to attain the wisdom necessary to lead a confident life free from inferiority feelings. Strange as it may seem, it can be done by a form of relaxation. When criticism or worries bring on irritability and anxieties, when tension mounts and problems seem insurmountable, periodic relaxation is one technique that reduces stress and can open the mind to unexpected solutions.

But how do you make yourself relax? Most of us find that commanding our bodies and minds to calm down just doesn't work. The brain continues to race and bodily tensions remain.

One approach to tension reduction should probably be mentioned here. It is a practical, scientific method that uses instruments and gauges to measure muscle tension, brain waves, and even finger temperature. It is called *biofeedback*. The advantage of this method is that people actually see the gauges that are connected to their bodies so they can continually monitor their bodies' functions. The gauges feed back the success or failure of their efforts at relaxing, thus enabling them to improve.

Such an attack upon stress is a bit complicated and may not be feasible for everyone. There is another way, however, which is the most time-tested of all. It is easy to master *provided* you have the key to its successful use. The process is simply one of relaxing and problem solving through meditation, but I am *not* referring to what is called Transcendental Meditation or T.M. Instead, I mean the time-honored Judeo-Christian meditation. Before describing the key to mastering it, it is important that you know how this type of meditation differs from other kinds.

When you hear the word *meditate*, perhaps your mind pictures a Buddha-like figure sitting cross-legged, staring vacantly into space. To me, that is not an appealing image.

To meditate has many shades of meaning, however. A dictionary will give you related verbs such as *to contemplate, muse, ponder, reflect, consider* and even the adjective, *pensive.* That's a pretty wide range of mental activity!

Nevertheless, we can think of meditation generally in one of two ways. There is the kind that several Eastern religions such as Hinduism and Buddhism practice. Hindus and Buddhists try to put all conscious thoughts from their minds, interested in divorcing themselves for a span of time from the realities of the world while in deep meditation. Their thinking turns internally, going deeper and deeper within the self until finally no thought at all remains. They become oblivious to their surroundings. To achieve this state requires much practice and patience.

It strikes me that such a state can be compared to that mysterious phenomenon of outer space called a *black hole.* I've heard it explained as a burnt-out star, which eons ago began collapsing into itself. It became smaller and smaller and at the same time heavier and heavier. Finally the tremendous weight from the force of its own gravity somehow pulled the dense mass inside out and it became a black hole.

Now, I know that's not a scientific explanation, and it's probably not a very accurate one either. It does, however, indicate what can happen when an object keeps pulling itself inward. That is not the sort of thing I am recommending!

Instead, let's look at Judeo-Christian meditation. To me, it is quite different. With it, there need be no attempt to stop the thought process. Keep the mind functioning! The key I previously mentioned to this type of meditation is to have something definite to think about—something positive and uplifting, not worrisome or disturbing in any way.

There are at least two general categories of subjects for the Christian and the Jew to meditate upon. One group consists of upward thoughts, and the other group of outward thoughts. Let me explain.

Judaism and Christianity trace their origins back to the patriarch, Abraham (as does the Islamic religion). However, Judaism and Christianity and to a large extent, Islam, differ from other major religions of the world in one momentous aspect—they teach that God is actually searching for each of us. Think about this for a moment. God stands, knocking at the door of our minds, seeking to come into our hearts and into our lives. We need do nothing to find God, except to let him in.

In other religions, man is the one doing the searching. It may be a search for God or it may be nothing more than working toward a release from the cycle of reincarnation and an escape into absolute and permanent oblivion. The teachers of those religions prescribe strict rules for the meditative process required to reach their goals. It is a long, rigorous, and ascetic process.

But for us, meditation can consist simply of opening the door for God to come in. This offers then an infinite number of his qualities to meditate upon, including the fact that his very search for us proves we must be of worth—we cannot be any kind of trash. These are upward thoughts.

The second grouping consists of outward thoughts. In contrast to the kind of meditation where a person seeks to go deeper and deeper into his or her own consciousness, Jews, Christians, or Muslims can cast their meditative eyes into the world about them.

Here again there are an unlimited amount of subjects. For one, we can reflect upon some fine qualities in our spouses. That's not only good for relaxation but for marital relations as well!

Another time, we could think about all the modern conveniences we enjoy that make life so much more pleasant than in earlier centuries where there were poor lighting, outdoor toilets, and cold, drafty housing.

But best of all, to give us a true and accurate sense of self-worth, we can meditate upon the needs of others we know, and think about ways to help them. A tried and true way to shake off depression and feelings of inferiority is to forget self and go about doing good for others. Such self-effacing activity must surely be a part of God's plan for each of us. By meditating on this subject and with prayer, it will become clear what path we are to follow. And then, gloom and despair fade gently away.

This need not happen in a charismatic mountaintop revelation, but it can occur more subtly. Have you ever been in a winter storm severe enough to disrupt your electrical service? If so, you know what sort of problems occur when the essentials of modern living do not work. Often after the storm, in the wee hours of the morning, you may awaken to the comforting awareness that power has again come into your home. Without fuss or fanfare, everything has begun to function again as it was planned to do. The heat switch on the thermostat has quietly turned up the gas in the furnace, and at the precise time, the fan softly beginning to move warm air throughout the rooms. The house seems to hum contentedly.

There has been no trauma, no shock, no wrenching displacement—just the quiet song of things going as planned. The problems of the storm fade away.

So it is that with upward and outward meditation, God's guidance and power can come quietly into any life. Then all the elements that make up that life will commence working again as God planned for them to do. The divine image somehow becomes present, and all fears and depression disappear as the night storm vanishes with the new day's dawn.

"For I know the plans I have for you, says the Lord, plans for welfare and not for evil, to give you a future and a hope" (Jer. 29:11).

Chapter Nine

WHY BOTHER TO BE ENTHUSIASTIC?
The Decisive Element in the Formula for Success

The prince strode regally through the crowd, smiling and nodding enthusiastically to all around him. He was the son of a great king with a proud heritage. His father's power and love backed him fully in all that he undertook. Why shouldn't he be enthusiastic?

Why should we not all be enthusiastic? We too have a great and imposing king as our father: a king so mighty that his power is without limits, a ruler so loving that he wills only good for each of his subjects.

And yet genuine enthusiasm is one of the most uncommon of all personality traits. How many wonderfully alive, warmly eager people do you know? Those who display zest and eagerness in their business dealings have a definite leg up on their competitors. As I've stated, our attitudes are probably the critical determinant in what we do with our lives. And enthusiasm may well be the very best possible foundation upon which to build such a winning attitude. It can be the decisive element in the formula for success. Do you doubt this? Listen!

"You can do anything if you have enthusiasm. . . . Enthusiasm is at the bottom of all progress. With it, there is accomplishment. Without it, there are only alibis" (Henry Ford).

"Enthusiasm is the propelling force that is necessary for climbing the ladder of success" (B. C. Forbes).

"Nothing great was ever achieved without enthusiasm" (Ralph Waldo Emerson).

"No man who is enthusiastic about his work has anything to fear from life" (Samuel Goldwyn).

I suppose it is possible to become too enthusiastic a person. After all, most everything can be overdone. Let's not confuse enthusiasm with the conceited urge to be a show-off. Theodore Roosevelt was probably our most ebullient president. But H. L. Mencken said about him, "Tempted sufficiently, he would sacrifice anything and everything to get applause."

There was the young lover who was so eager for his distant sweetheart's love that he wrote to her every day. That takes a lot of zeal! But what happened? After a year, she married the postman!

Mae West, on the other hand, did not think you could overdo anything that was gratifying. She supposedly said, "Too much of a good thing can be wonderful."

With all the material comforts in today's American society, why should there not be more enthusiastic people? There are numerous reasons I suppose—poor health, death of loved ones, alcoholism. But for the average individual in normal circumstances, I can think of three especially potent pressures or influences that can dampen anyone's zest.

The first influence is the instant news that we receive regularly throughout the day from newspapers, radios, and television. Indeed, there are some radio and TV channels broadcasting nothing but news. And what does the news consist of today? The biggest part, by far, is depressing. Our minds are filled with reports of natural disasters, manmade sufferings, and dire predictions as to what is to come. "It's enough to give anyone the 'willies,' " a wise lady once said to me.

Well, we can't ignore what's going on in the world, but we don't have to try to carry all the burdens on our own shoulders. Of course, we should do what we can to relieve the suffering of others, but it is of no help to anyone to go around saddened by all of the misery that does exist and probably always has existed.

Before the invention of the telegraph, it took weeks or even months for disaster news from far-off lands to reach our shores. Today we have it instantly in our living rooms via satellite. And that's a telling difference.

Nevertheless it is possible to keep enthusiasm alive even today. God is still on the bridge and in command of the world. All that seems to be going so wrong now may eventually turn out for the best. The long view of history is what counts, and we should focus on it.

Our former ambassador to Switzerland, Shelby Cullom Davis, was a self-made man. Starting from very little he earned so much wealth that when he was in his fifties he was able to give Princeton University the largest financial gift his alma mater had ever received from a living alumnus.

At a dinner in his honor, Davis was asked how he was able to accomplish this. He was quoted as saying, "I owe it all to the study of history. For history teaches us that waves are more important than ripples, and tides are more important than waves."

Enthusiastic people keep their eyes on the tides. They do not choose to permit the daily ripples of news to depress them. As children of the great king, they are confident in their father's power to control all events for ultimate good, and they can relax, at ease with that thought.

The second pressure that can wither enthusiasm is severe financial problems. If you read chapter 4, you know that I think the steady practice of tithing greatly increases the odds *against* such difficulties. But the fact is, unfortunately, that most people do not tithe.

It strikes me as obvious that prudent money management is essential in order to be a bona fide, unpretendingly enthusiastic person. John Savage, the author of the book, *The Easy Sale*, has also tied money management directly with business success. He once said, "The first most important trait for success is that a person be able to manage his own affairs."

It is possible, of course, to put on a false front before others and to appear cheerful—at least for awhile. It seems unlikely, however, that someone whose debts are piling up and whose financial records are in disarray could hope to play that role for long. It is essential that credit be under tight control and all debt repayment managed within a realistic budget.

Happily, in most cities there are professional debt counseling services—often not-for-profit community service organizations. With the latter, there is usually no charge for their helpful advice. These organizations can be found in the Yellow Pages directory, perhaps under "Financial Planning" or "Debt Consolidation" or "Debt Adjusters." Their role is to guide a financially strapped person or family back onto the road toward ultimate solvency. They can advise on debt consolidation and probably the most important factor of all, realistic budgeting of the family's income and expenses.

No one can be full of zest while being constantly dunned. There may also be a feeling of guilt because we all know that when bills can't be paid promptly, others suffer. Most people don't like to have that on their conscience.

A guilty conscience is the third pressure that influences enthusiasm in a negative way. No matter how much it is repressed or denied, guilt is a burden to the human spirit. It can well up unexpectedly to drown even the happiest moment. It can filter in from the subconscious like the evening mist from a fog bank far out at sea. There is always a trace of it in some corner of the mind that shuttles out at the most inappropriate times. It is a depressant that lowers the intensity of enthusiasm.

Put yourself in this situation: You were the chief executive officer of a business firm that went into bankruptcy and subsequently failed. Many people have been hurt by its demise. Employees lost their jobs, stockholders their investments, and creditors the amounts owed them.

You were considered the one most responsible for their plight. As a conscientious person, you go over and over in your mind the events that led to your company's failure. You ask yourself questions like these: Was failure inevitable, or was there more that I might have done? Did I work as hard as I might have? Was I an incompetent manager? If so, was it because I was lazy or drinking too heavily, or was it that my ingenuity and even my brain power were simply inadequate for my responsibilities?

Many times an honest answer will produce guilt. But, it need not damage one's life indefinitely.

One of the most reassuring stories in the New Testament for me has always been Peter's denial of Jesus. You remember that Simon Peter, in an exalted moment, previously had declared to Jesus, "You are the Christ, the Son of the living God" (Matthew 16:16).

And Jesus answered him, "Blessed are you, Simon

107

Bar-Jona! . . . And I tell you, you are Peter [*petros* = rock], and on this rock I will build my church, and the powers of death shall not prevail against it" (Matthew 16:17-18).

Imagine the thrill that must have gone through Peter when he heard those words. He was the one Jesus was counting on to be as steadfast as a mighty rock, the very foundation of his earthly church. What an awesome responsibility for a mortal to be given. But in a very short time that rock seemed to crumble. The night of Jesus' trial Peter *three times* denied that he even knew Jesus. Then apparently, he fled like a coward into hiding until news of Jesus' resurrection reached him.

The outcome of this story is what reassures me when I have failed in some duty. Jesus forgave Peter for his craven desertion. Over the centuries many have wondered how a rugged individual like Peter who had lived in close companionship with Jesus himself could have had such a moment of weakness. Would not his guilt afterward have been crushing? Thank God that someone as trusted as Simon Peter *did* fail so miserably and yet was forgiven so completely that his guilt was both erased and forgotten! That fact and the acceptance of it give heart to those bearing a burden of guilt. It allows eagerness and verve to return and with them the open road to future success.

In a shopping center near my home are two stores. I have stopped trading with one because the young people behind the counter are so indifferent to their customers. They show little interest in anything as they perform their routines like robots. I don't think they know the meaning of the word *enthusiasm*. It's also apparent that management has not tried to teach them good customer relations.

The other establishment is a drug store. The man who founded it is now deceased, but he left it in good hands. It is an actual pleasure to shop there. The saleswoman behind the cosmetic counter is one of the reasons I like to go in. I know her name is Scottie because she usually introduces herself to her customers and is attentive to their needs. She is not a young girl, but she is certainly young at heart.

Now I don't buy much in the way of cosmetics! But I never go into that store without stopping by to say hello to Scottie. Her sweet, enthusiastic manner brightens my day. And I think to myself, she is certainly working as hard as those uncaring teenagers with no personality, yet she's also having a lot of fun in her job. Why don't they get smart and try putting more of themselves into their work the way she does? They come in contact with many men and women each week. Some of those men and women could well be looking for a bright, eager youngster for their business. But no one will be attracted to a dull person.

One of the more enthusiastic older women I can remember was a volunteer guide and lecturer in a museum on Nantucket, a captivating island off the coast of Cape Cod with interesting shops and several quaint museums. One day my wife and I entered one of them just as this woman was beginning her tour. We followed her around the place, fascinated by her knowledge of the exhibits and by the way she threw herself into telling about them.

She came to a rather peculiar chair with ropes and pulleys attached to it. She told us we were in for a surprise and then proceeded to describe this seat as a "potty chair." She said that in the old whaling days the captains often took their wives along. At sea they would put the women in the potty chair and swing them out over the side of the ship.

"Now, wait a minute," I thought. "This gal is really getting carried away!" I couldn't believe what I was hearing. Then it dawned on me. This lady had a typical Boston accent. When she said "potty chair," she meant "party chair." These chairs were used not for sanitation purposes, but to transfer a wife from one ship for a short visit or party with the wife on another ship when they chanced to meet at sea.

If I had been looking for a top-flight tour director or lecturer for my business, I would have tried to hire that energetic senior citizen on the spot, in spite of her accent!

What do you think of as the antonym of *enthusiastic?* You could say, *disinterested* or *placid* or even *phlegmatic.* I believe I would choose *cynical.* The cynic might ask, "Why be enthusiastic—why put out that much energy? Just play it cool, or you might be considered naïve."

Well, there is also an answer to that from a physical health standpoint. According to the April 1984 issue of *Psychology Today*, recent medical and psychiatric research suggests that cynicism can lead to earlier death, particularly from heart disease. The article goes into some detail to explain the apparent connection between cynicism and death. An intriguing aspect of these results to me is that the writer of the seventeenth chapter of Proverbs long ago came to much the same conclusion. You may remember the statement, "A cheerful heart is a good medicine, but a downcast spirit dries up the bones" (17:22). Positive thinking people who are vitally alive often are unusually healthy!

There is something about that kind of person that warms the heart, even when you don't agree with them. They may make mistakes, but at least they *do* something with their lives. They are too brimful of energy ever to be lukewarm on any subject. In the first century following Jesus' death and resurrection, John of Patmos writing to the church at Sardis forwarded to them these words of Jesus: "You are neither cold nor hot. Would that you *were* cold or hot! So, because you are lukewarm . . . I will spew you out of my mouth" (Revelation 3:15-16, italics added).

We are told that we are all children of God (I John 3:1). So why shouldn't we be enthusiastic? Like any beloved son of a great king, our father's power and love are there to back us fully in all that we undertake. Our lives can be rich and rewarding and our friends warm and responsive.

Enthusiastic people, you see, have fun instead of fear, songs instead of sighs. Like the magnificent first movement of Beethoven's Seventh Symphony, they exude vitality and self-confidence. Mistakes they make, as do all of us, but just as Simon Peter rose above his blundering and the terrible guilt that must have followed, the enthusiastic soon are able to find new strength and to hit the high road to ultimate success. The odds are exceedingly long in their favor!

Chapter Ten

GREED: BANE OR BLESSING?

In the last chapter we talked about enthusiasm—the uplift and the impetus that gives spice to our lives and vigor to our actions. When enthusiasm is joined to the normal desire to make money, the path to financial success is usually shortened. The aspiration to possess wealth is probably instinctive. Most people have the ambition to make money. If this inclination is channeled in the proper way, it can be a blessing to many. It is healthy when the eagerness to acquire material riches is not *excessive.*

We call it greed when someone has an inordinate craving for acquiring much more money and material things than he needs. For example, after the wife of a friend of mine divorced him, he told me, "My goal now is to become the richest man in town." In reality, his wounded vanity was probably the fuel for his greed and not solely a compulsion for more and more money.

Obviously, there is more than one cause of greediness. Vanity is one of the principal ones. If you are driving up the coast of California, be sure to stop at San Simeon to tour the famous castle that the newspaper mogul, William Randolph Hearst, built in the 1920s. After his initial land purchase, Hearst had the obsession to own all of the land he could see in every direction from his hilltop mansion. As that hill is quite high, his view encompassed thousands of acres, which he eventually acquired. There is nothing particularly wrong with amassing land. But in this case, it was far beyond any rational need and probably merely to satisfy his vanity so that he could say to his friends, "Look out in any direction. Whatever you see is mine!"

Many people who are considered strong and powerful are actually motivated by the need to prove themselves to others. The higher their title and the more power and civic prestige they have, the easier it is for them to accept themselves as someone of worth. But too often such self-acceptance never quite seems to come and that lack keeps their flame of greed burning.

The womanizer who attempts to outdo Casanova in his sexual conquests may also be driven by a similar desire to prove something about himself, in this case, his masculinity.

Then, of course, we all know the glutton for food. You may not realize it, but a greedy desire for food, especially at bargain prices, can produce extraordinary energy as a story from my college days at Princeton University attests.

There were four of us living in a suite of dormitory rooms. One day we read in a New York newspaper an advertisement for a brand new gourmet restaurant just opening in an affluent east side area of Manhattan. The ad said that during the first week of operations the restaurant would give a 90 percent discount to the party of no more than six who were first in line when the doors opened for dinner.

Princeton is one hour away by car or train from New York. By the time we saw the ad there were only two more days left in that week. But that large discount spoke directly to our greed, so the next afternoon all four of us were on our way into New York in a car belonging to one of my roommates.

There was, at that time, a long standing prohibition against having an automobile at Princeton. Anyone caught during the school year driving his own car nearer to Princeton than his home was summarily expelled—no explanations allowed!

This particular roommate was from Chicago, but during our last year he had driven his car from Chicago to Princeton and stored it in a garage on the outskirts of town. When we decided to drive to the city, we knew we were taking a chance, but our heads were filled with the vision of what would take place if we were first in line. Before the Second World War, a good dinner could be had for less than three dollars and I looked forward to ordering the most expensive entree on the menu. And champagne! I may have tasted champagne before, but if so, it undoubtedly was a cheap vintage. We were going to order the best. It was possible that our bill could even reach the then astronomical sum of one hundred dollars! But even that unthinkable amount with the discount would only come to ten dollars. Dividing that by the four of us, we would have to pay only $2.50 apiece! Each of us affirmed that we had that much in our pockets.

We parked the car on a side street and reached the restaurant a good half hour before the doorman showed up. We were elated when he arrived and verified that we were first in line and would indeed be charged only 10 percent of whatever we ordered. "BUT," he continued—and here our hearts sank—"you fellows didn't read the ad very carefully. It said that there must be at least one woman in the party."

What a predicament! We held a hasty conference. Jack, from Chicago, did know a girl in the city, and he quickly phoned her, but no luck. Then we flipped a coin. One stayed to hold our place in line while the rest of us fanned out to see if we could entice some female to join us in the thirty minutes the doorman had said he would allow us.

I chose to go into a couple of nearby hotel lobbies. It's hard for me now to believe that I actually did this, but I went up to several young ladies sitting in those lobbies. I asked them if they would let me explain something to them. None of them would. I was rebuffed! Nevertheless, the gluttonous vision that was slipping rapidly away drove me on. Desperately I began stopping women on the sidewalk—young, pretty ones at first, but soon just any age as long as it was female.

Very soon my time was up. I hurried back to the restaurant hoping against hope that my more sophisticated roommates might have had better luck. But no, we were expelled from the line and wandered dejectedly back to the car, our hotheaded craving unsatisfied.

The story doesn't end there. As we turned into the block where the car was parked, to our consternation we saw it surrounded by a small crowd of people including two or three policemen. I was certain that we had been caught—our disobedience of the car rule uncovered. I had visions of returning home in disgrace to an irate father. And, but for the grace of God, that is what could have easily happened. We learned that a driver had lost control of his car and had crashed into the side of the one parked directly ahead of ours. The police were trying to locate the owner of that car before they had it towed away. If the careening vehicle had struck a few feet sooner, our names would have been recorded and eventually reported to the college. The desire to eat so well for so little had nearly cost us a college degree.

No harm came from that particular exercise in greed. On the positive side, I will say that ever since, I've had a sort of admiration for any man who can pick up a strange woman!

I guess that relatively few people are immune from the temptation of getting something for little or nothing. I know that my own father, whom I greatly respected, fell into that trap when he was a young man. In this case, however, he later told me that he had benefitted from his experience. Here is what happened.

A year or so after he married, an older friend of his from California came to spend a day or two at our house. Robert Brown was on his way to New York by train to close the sale of thousands of acres of land in the San Joaquin Valley in central California. He had long been a mentor of my father's and was a completely trustworthy man. He and a few other investors had been buying this land for several years. Now they had located a buyer, and Robert Brown would complete the sale in a few days in New York. The profit would be substantial.

Brown told my father that he could buy some of this land at the original cost. Then in a few days he would reap a considerable profit. Now please note, my father's money was not needed. The land had already been purchased. He was not contributing to this venture in a meaningful way as Brown and his other associates had done. His old friend was simply giving up part of his own profit—a most generous act!

So, my father went to his bank and borrowed every cent he could, mortgaging whatever could be mortgaged, bursting to grab all that he could of this offer. I don't know how much money was involved, but it was enough to buy two sections of that land, 1,280 acres. My father was then deeply in debt but supremely confident that very shortly he would be rich!

Robert Brown went to New York, arriving on a weekend. The prospective buyer of the land met him and took him to his country home until the following Monday when the deal was to be closed. That night his host and wife took him out to dinner. He was dancing with his hostess when she said, "Mr. Brown, you've had a long trip here from California, how are you feeling?" He replied, "I never felt better in my life," whereupon he dropped dead upon the dance floor!

The upshot of this whole affair was that the sale was never consummated. My father was stuck with both that land and a heavy debt for a great many years. Those two sections of wheat land produced mostly taxes for him, and he did not find another buyer until World War II, some thirty years later!

I'm sure he must have been panic-stricken at the news of Robert Brown's death. But many years later he told me that the heavy burden of debt forced him to work harder than he might otherwise have done. He attributed a good part of his success to that early hurdle that he was forced to jump. His one-time greed and the worries it caused turned out in this case to be a blessing in disguise.

There is a natural human urge to acquire wealth. Who hasn't dreamed of striking it rich someday? In business we praise the ambition, the drive, the aggressiveness, and ingenuity of those who keenly desire to get ahead—to make something of themselves and to make money. If such as this is greed, then greed can be a blessing. As I've said, humans have always struggled to possess—land, power, and gold. Such striving is quite likely essential for progress. Robert Browning, in his poem "Andrea del Sarto," praised what Shakespeare termed "vaulting ambition," by declaring, "Ah, but a man's reach should exceed his grasp, / Or what's a heaven for?"

Before the Industrial Revolution there was little wealth, and only those who controlled people or territory had it. Too often those could be acquired only by force, principally by warring on some neighboring tribe or nation. Unfortunately in many countries today, force is the means to wealth for those of the ruling clique. Thus greed in such cases is a bane because the freedom of others is sacrificed for it.

It is the free-enterprise, capitalist system that channels the compulsion to acquire into positive good for others. This is not because of any inherent altruism in entrepreneurs or in businessmen but because of the way our system functions. Let me illustrate.

I have a friend who, no more than a dozen years ago, bought an obscure little manufacturing company. He recently sold it for twenty-five million dollars. How did he do it? Very simply. He expanded his product line to appeal to more buyers, and he reduced costs by more efficient design. The result of his efforts benefitted a great many consumers. But I think I am safe in assuming that he did not buy this business in the first place just to befriend the public. No, I feel certain his approach to this purchase was more economic than humanitarian. He must have carefully examined the past financial results, plus market surveys, and concluded that with his energy, his ambition, and his engineering skill, he could better manage that business to make it grow into something extremely profitable.

Along the way, of course, more jobs were created and many employees raised to higher paying positions. People across the country buying his products were served with better wares at reduced cost. Even if you should insist on calling him a greedy man, which he is not, that greed under our economic system produced good results or blessings for untold numbers of others as well as for himself.

Those who have attained power either through their political office or their wealth have to deal with the use of that power. If they manage it in a way that contributes to the overall good, then the ambition that won them their power was a blessing. Humans tend to move in the direction of their thoughts. If inordinate greed rules their thinking, they will use whatever money and influence they have principally to serve themselves.

Nevertheless, anyone in business who truly desires to benefit others as well as himself must first survive economically. His company must remain profitable. There must be a drive for those profits, if there are to be benefits to others.

It takes maturity to walk the fine line between avarice and ambition. Professor Lynn Taylor, the executive director of the Kansas School of Religion at the University of Kansas, has written, "Maturity depends upon some canons of discipline to serve a higher purpose. And humankind is capable of that. Maturity lies in the direction of words like *sharing, perspective, responsibility.* Immaturity is defined with actions such as *exploit, use, manipulate.*"

Earlier in this century a man named John R. Mott became internationally known for his rapport with businessmen, although he was involved strictly with charitable activities. For some years he was the general secretary of the National Council of the YMCAs of America. In a book describing his accomplishments (*Dr. John R. Mott: World Citizen*, by Basil Mathews), Mott is quoted as saying in 1928, "Money has power to multiply greatly one's opportunities, influence and fruitfulness. With equal truth it multiplies one's responsibilities, and duties, and in the possession and use of money, as of any great power, one's risks and perils are enormously increased."

Jesus knew well the risks and perils involved with money. In the sixth chapter of Matthew, he said, "No one can serve two masters. . . . You cannot serve God and mammon. . . . But seek first his kingdom and his righteousness, and all these things shall be yours as well."

In the past when I have deliberated over a financial decision, I have asked three questions: "Am I planning this for no other reason than to make money? Would it be unfair to anyone? Would customers or the public receive any benefits?"

Then I ask myself this crucial question: "If I were to die

tonight and stand before some heavenly judge, would I be glad or sad that I took this action?" Since we have no idea when we'll be called before that judge, we should consider this possibility in all we do. I'm sure you realize that what we say belongs to us is really just a loan. I don't *own* my house or my farm. I don't *own* any stocks or bonds. They have been loaned to me. In banking terms, it is a *callable loan*, or a *demand note*. That means that all worldly goods, life, health, even my wife and children, can be instantly demanded from me and I will find them repossessed immediately.

No one knows the terms of his own note. It may be long- or short-term. All we know is that at some point all notes will be called. In view of this, greed can be properly assessed. Ambition and aggressiveness, yes, if for a worthy purpose. But thumbs down on actions that are excessively selfish and hurtful to others.

The proud and the arrogant deny dependence upon God. They believe in their own abilities to such an extent that they disdain the idea of any indebtedness to him. Often, to prove their cleverness they seek to stockpile insatiably. They acknowledge no reliance upon God and because of that, they well may be bringing to pass their own downfall. It is written:

"Take heed lest you forget the Lord your God . . . lest, when you have eaten and are full, and have built goodly houses and live in them . . . and your silver and gold is multiplied, and all that you have is multiplied, then your heart be lifted up, and you forget the Lord your God . . . . Beware lest you say in your heart, 'My power and the might of my hand have gotten me this wealth.' You shall remember the Lord your God, for it is he who gives you power to get wealth. . . . And if you forget the Lord your God . . . I solemnly warn you this day that you shall surely perish" (Deuteronomy 8:11-14, 17-19).

Chapter Eleven

ALL THINGS WORK TOGETHER
Learning to Trust

When the gods wish to punish us they answer our prayers.
Oscar Wilde

It was early spring in 1945. Daylight was filtering through the thick tropical jungle of Manus Island off the northern coast of New Guinea. Sweltering in my bunk at the Navy barracks I had slept fitfully. Now it was time to dress and begin another leg on the long trip by air from Honolulu to rejoin my ship, the *U.S.S. Luce*, operating somewhere in the Philippines.

There was no regular transportation service. I had to hitchhike on cargo planes, going wherever they were heading so long as it was westward out over the vast Pacific Ocean.

The night before, two Air Corps officers had arrived on Manus in a twin engine DC-3. They had agreed to take me to Tacloban, on the northern edge of the Philippine island of Leyte. By the time the sun was up, I was riding in a jeep through the steaming jungle to a clearing where a frightfully short runway had been cleared.

As we approached the clearing, drops of water fell from the humid vines hanging in strands between the giant trees. I could picture Tarzan swinging through the middle terraces of those trees and could almost hear his ape-man call. Then the shout of the pilot brought me back to the reality of war.

"Hurry up, Jones," he yelled. "We're already running late!"

I rushed up the steps and dropped into an uncomfortable

bucket seat. He and the copilot took their places and without a second's warm-up of those damp engines, off we flew over the nearly impenetrable jungle.

After intermediate stops, we landed the next morning at Tacloban. Again I was urged to hurry because there was only one plane a day from there to Leyte Gulf where my ship might be found. It was only a hundred yards or so to the tin shed that served as a terminal. I remember breathing a prayer that I would be in time. But as I floundered to the counter with my heavy sea-bag, the officer in charge pointed out the back door to the runway and said, "Look, there goes your plane just taking off."

I can see it now—the lift-off and the lowering of the wing as it made a graceful left turn to the south toward Leyte Gulf. I suddenly realized how tired I was.

My discomfiture became more acute when I learned there was really no place for me to wait for the next morning's plane. Instead I was advised to board an open landing craft that was soon leaving for my destination. It would take all day by boat instead of a short half-hour by plane.

It was one of the longest days of my life. There was no room for me in the wheelhouse of that boat. I sat in the broiling sun all day trying vainly to find a little shade behind coils of line. I was too uncomfortable to nap, and there was nothing to read. There was a limited supply of drinking water, and it was hot. I don't remember having any food. But what bothered me most was that God had not answered my prayer. It would have been easy for him to have delayed that plane for two minutes or so, and I blamed him for not doing this. I was suffering in the heat because he would not do what I had asked of him. I even recalled Jesus' words, "Ask and ye shall receive."

"Baloney," I thought.

Eventually we arrived at a base in Leyte Gulf. Bone-weary, I managed to find a barracks where I learned the earthshaking news that the plane from Tacloban had crashed, killing all on board. Without realizing it, I had prayed that morning for my own death!

Only four short years before, I had been reading *The Rubáiyát* of Omar Khayyám in a college English course. One verse now came back to me. Do you remember these famous lines?

> *Ah Love! could you and I with Him conspire*
> *To grasp this Sorry Scheme of Things entire,*
> *Would not we shatter it to bits—and then*
> *Remold it nearer to the Heart's Desire!*

I had always felt pretty much that same way. If I were God, I would certainly do things differently. For one thing, the good guys would always win and live a long, long, time. The baddies would always lose. But then, if that were so, would my life have been spared? I realized that the chances were good that those killed in the crash had been leading better lives than I had to that point.

And take the matter of Jesus' crucifixion. If I had had God's power, I wouldn't have stood for that! I would have zapped those Roman soldiers and had Jesus step down from the cross and *then* be lifted up to heaven. In that way there would have been plenty of historical proof that he was indeed what Christians claim him to be. It would then follow logically that all peoples would soon become believers.

Years later reading the Old Testament, I realized that such clear-cut demonstrations of God's miraculous assistance to the righteous had seldom had any lasting effect. This was so even for those who were right there as witnesses.

There is that story concerning the rebellion of Korah and his cohorts against Moses, described in the sixteenth chapter of Numbers. In spite of God's obvious support of Moses and his leadership of the Israelites, Korah and some others dared to challenge his right to direct them. Now just think—they had observed Moses stretching out his hand over the Red Sea and the parting of its waters so that they could safely pass. They had seen manna or bread come from heaven and water pour from rocks at Moses' command. And yet their murmurings against him increased until finally Korah chose to defy Moses to his face.

Here is the part where God acted exactly the way Omar Khayyám and I would have. He not only struck down Korah and his henchmen, but he caused the earth to open up and swallow them so that they perished from among the congregation.

You'll remember, however, that the very next morning the people were muttering and murmuring against Moses again, even though they had just seen God's divine wrath. Consequently, I came to the reluctant conclusion that God's often unfathomable ways were undoubtedly better than any simplistic method old Omar or I could possibly devise.

The Bible recounts other instances of God showing his all-powerful hand to uphold the virtuous and to destroy the wrongdoer. But its effect upon faith was seldom permanent.

For another thriller, read in I Kings 18:37 how the prophet Elijah stood before the king, the prophets of Baal, and the people of Israel and prayed aloud, "Answer me, O Lord, answer me that this people may know that thou, O Lord, art God, and that thou hast turned their heart back." Read how fire descended from heaven and consumed not only the sacrifice that was there but even the stones and the water that had drenched the altar. Then read on to see that even such fantastic proof of God's existence and his power did absolutely no good.

So, maybe God does know what he is doing. Perhaps there really is a very good reason for what he allows to happen, even though we may not be capable of recognizing it. In fact, we may be praying earnestly that it not happen. Probably all of us can recall a time when we later thanked God for not giving us whatever we had prayed for.

But what about the horrible disasters that occur from time to time? Surely they can't produce anything good? Well, let me tell you that no philosopher or deep thinker that I have read or heard has ever answered that question to my complete satisfaction. I'm afraid that our mental capacities and our spiritual insight are far too limited to do more than catch glimpses now and then of the infinite wisdom behind all of God's universe.

And yet from time to time we do see the flash of God's own hand in the aftermath of tragedy, preparing the way for beneficial change to those whose love and trust do not falter. All who have had such experiences know that it takes a mighty leap of faith to say that even in tragedy, God is working for good.

Take the 1981 collapse of a skywalk in a crowded Kansas City hotel. Just over a hundred people were killed when it fell and more than two hundred injured. It seemed that nearly everyone I knew had some friend or loved one involved in that calamity. At that time, I wouldn't have given a plugged nickel for anything good ever coming from that disaster.

But now that time has passed there have been some positive results, and here are several I am aware of:

- All across the country serious thought has been given to improved and more frequent inspections of buildings and bridges. As a consequence, it is conceivable that in future years many more lives will be saved than were lost in Kansas City.

- Architects and engineers have learned additional facts from this collapse, which will translate into the safer design of future structures.

- The building inspection department of the city of Kansas City was shaken up and reorganized so there is now greater assurance that new construction will be built in exact accordance with plans and specifications.

- A young single woman seeking God's will for her life was in the hotel that night. Uninjured herself, she was emotionally shaken by the devastation all about her. Her thoughts continued to dwell on the anguish she had observed, and her sleep was racked by nightmares. Her wise father suggested that she lose herself in service to others. So she set out to visit all the injured who were still in hospitals. In one she met a man grieving deeply over his wife's death in the skywalk crash. She continued her hospital visits, and over many months they fell in love and were married. Their life together now is bright with good promise for the future.

- Finally, there was the unknown man who was brought out from the hotel uninjured. He was not allowed to go back in search of his wife. So he stood as close as possible to the stretchers bringing out the dead and injured, peering intently into each face. A newspaper reported him agonizing aloud, "My whole life is still in there!" Now I wonder how many men reading that tortured statement thought of their wives. I'm sure there were many who imagined themselves in that situation. "If my wife is brought out dead, there goes my whole life. What I would give to have her back again! I would gladly say to her, 'I'll never complain about those little habits of yours that annoyed me. Having you alive is the most important thing in my life. From now on our married life is going to be much better.' "

Who knows how many marriages were improved because of one man's haunting declaration in the newspaper!

Many deeply religious people affirm the truth of this quotation from Paul's letter to the Romans: "We know that in everything God works for good with those who love him, who are called according to his purpose" (Romans 8:28). It may well be for those who love and trust him implicitly that everything does turn out for the best. We can't really prove this, of course. There is no way in this life of knowing whether every tragedy that happens will produce good. For my part, I am content to accept the thought of the Jewish Rabbinic tradition that says that all things *can* work together for good.

I can't even guess why some things are allowed to happen. But I firmly believe that the odds are very high, indeed, that good can and will come from them if those involved have the kind of faith that says, "Somehow, in some way, whatever has happened to me, God can use it for my benefit if I will just continue to trust him."

A friend of mine challenged me recently on this point. "What you are saying," he said, "is that the Christian faith produces a can't-lose situation. I don't go along with that idea because too many bad things happen to too many good people."

"Well," I acknowledged, "no one knows all the answers. But, you have just given me the best definition of Christian faith I have ever heard. You said it is a Can't-Lose situation. I like that!"

Christians who dedicate themselves to the instructions of the Bible, who develop absolute confidence in its promises, can know with certainty that no matter what happens, God is working all things together for good. If we had divine insight, we could understand why seemingly bad things happen. But we'll never have anything like that kind of discernment, in this life, at any rate.

Consequently, patience for the long run is also a requisite. We in this modern age are often impatient. Like the prayer of the harried individual who implored, "God, I need to be more patient. Please grant me patience, and do it right away!"

Contrast such chafing with the self-control and resignation of the pioneers. It is said that one family started from the Eastern seaboard for California with a team of oxen to pull their covered wagon with a baby ox trailing behind. In the Midwest one of the oxen died. So the family stopped, cleared a little land, built a cabin, and waited there until the baby ox grew up. They could then start off again. Today, some of us are upset if we miss one turn of a revolving door!

When my grandfather, R. B. Jones, entered the general insurance business in 1889, there was only one product to sell, and that was an insurance policy against fire damage. There was no such thing as windstorm, burglary, liability, or workers' compensation insurance. After he made a sale, the policy was written out in longhand in his office. Then he would go out in back, hitch up his wagon, and drive for maybe an hour to deliver the policy. He worked very long hours six days a week and probably some on Sundays when my grandmother would let him. Our work today for the most part has been squeezed into much shorter hours. But as with a gas when its volume is compressed, the pressure on it increases. So with too many of us, the hours are shorter, but the pressure of an ordinary working day is immense.

We can't go riding slowly along in a buggy pondering on the meaning of the things that have happened to us. If those things appear to be bad, well, that's the way we accept them. They *are* bad as far as we are concerned, and even good churchgoing folks too often do not have time to meditate on how the hand of God may be trying to lead them into something better.

A newspaper columnist last year wrote a gloomy article considering the question of how our lives are determined by luck. His conclusion was that everything is a matter of luck. Whether a person is rich or poor, gifted or flawed, happy or not, all of that is a matter of luck. Who has not felt that way at certain times?

This journalist obviously would not credit God with guiding the lives of those who place their trust in him. If he believes in a god at all, it must be in one who perhaps set the world in motion but then withdrew to remain forever aloof from mankind.

Two young men applied to an Ivy League college that both their fathers had attended. These two fathers prayed about this matter. One asked God to have his son admitted to that special college. The other prayed that his son be accepted at the college of God's choice.

Both boys were turned down. They had to take their second choice. The first father was furious. He swore that he would never give another cent to his old school as long as he lived.

The second father gave thanks, trusting that the Lord was steering his son to the place where good things were in store for him. Perhaps there at that second choice school he would meet the girl who would become his wife. Perhaps he would be influenced by just the right professor into the career that God had in mind for him from the beginning. And perhaps at the college of his first choice none of those things would have happened.

As a matter of fact, that is precisely the way it did turn out for the second young man. Married bliss and the inspiration for a successful career were there waiting for him. Human eyes cannot see such things. But human trust in God and in his word brought it all together. As the Bible says:

> "For the word of the Lord is upright;
>   and all his work is done in faithfulness.
> He loves righteousness and justice;
>   the earth is full of the steadfast love of the Lord. . . .
> Let thy steadfast love be upon us,
>   even as we hope in thee" (Psalm 33:4, 5, 22).

Chapter Twelve

DARE TO BE DIFFERENT

There is a small unincorporated community in Davidson County, Tennessee, called Amqui. In the old days of railroading, it had importance. Those days are long past, and country singer Johnny Cash has purchased the quaint railway station and moved it to his estate.

Amqui is an unusual name, to say the least. And the way they tell it, that name came about in an even stranger way. When Amqui was settled by railroaders, their foreman told them to pick out a name for the place, and do it "damn quick." So, they named the town Damquik.

In time, some of the more conservative folks cleaned the name up a bit by eliminating the first and last letters. Thus was created Amqui.

At any rate, Amqui was once a switching point on the Louisville and Nashville line. If the switchman moved the track six inches to the right, the trains from the south would thunder past on the way to Louisville and Cincinnati. If the track was moved only six inches to the left, the trains went to St. Louis or Chicago—an enormous variance in their final destination brought about by a matter of only a few inches.

The horse that wins the Kentucky Derby each year runs that race in only a few seconds less than the slowest horse in the pack. Yet that slender difference produces the winner's wreath.

Today as you finish this book you may be at a switching

point in your personal history. A resolve on your part to make a relatively small adjustment in basic priorities could turn you toward successes now only dreamed of.

If you will look back over the preceding chapters, you may discover where such an adjustment could be helpful. The table of contents gives an easy-to-use check-off list for a quick review.

Chapter 1

Am I satisfied at this point with the overall success of my life? And if financial prosperity has been attained, what about self-esteem? Mark Twain said, "A man cannot be comfortable without his own approval." If I do not have self-respect, possibly all that is needed to restore it is an alteration in my thinking or in my actions.

Chapter 2

One of these ten business mistakes could be my problem. Why not carefully review them to find out?

Chapter 3

How well do I handle problems? Do I stand up under stress? How often do I think about and act upon special promises made by God to all who will listen and believe them?

Chapter 4

If money problems are still a big worry, am I actually giving away 10 percent of my income? Why not test it for a year?

Chapter 5

Have I made out a personal code of ethics? Do I review it as a road map to keep me on the right track?

Chapter 6

When I am weary and discouraged, am I able to get my thinking back into the positive mode? Have I thought about the Smorgasbord Theory?

Chapter 7

Is fear still too prominent in my life? Have I memorized the often overlooked Bible verse on this subject?

Chapter 8

How often do I take the time to relax and meditate? Without meditation, I may not be able to discern God's plan for my life.

Chapter 9

How high is the level of my enthusiasm? What is the condition of my conscience? If enthusiasm regularly runs high, then there can't be much to worry about. I remind myself that I am the beloved child of a great king.

Chapter 10

What about my ambition—is it a bane or a blessing to others? Am I trying to serve both God and mammon?

Chapter 11

How strong is my belief that in everything God works for good? Is life for me a "can't-lose situation"? Do I need to reinforce my love and my trust in him?

If you are satisfied with your answers, the odds are favorable that you have indeed dared to be different. You are not a sheep, following where others lead. You make your own

decisions and with God's help, you are making your life count
for something.

You can feel only pity for a man I'll call Sam, although he is
a nice guy. He makes himself pleasing to those about him. He
is the assistant to the owner of a small business and
well-known in his trade. Because of his good nature, he
recently was elected president of his local trade association. It
is largely an honorary position, and he anticipated no
problems. To his dismay a divisive issue arose, and naturally,
many looked to Sam for some display of leadership. But at a
membership meeting he refused to take a position. He said in
so many words, "I've never offended anybody in my life. I
don't ever want to. So you vote the way you want, and
however the vote comes out, that's the direction I'll lead you."

Now what kind of leadership is that? This man would not
risk being different. He wanted nothing more than to stay
submerged in the mainstream of opinion. By not forthrightly
stating his own opinions, he thought he would be secure. But
he was mistaken. The effective leadership of his group passed
into other hands and he was left behind, as Sir Walter Scott
put it, "unwept, unhonor'd, and unsung."

But now let me tell you about someone of a different sort,
someone who set out to become an uncommon man. He is
Ewing M. Kauffman, chairman of the board and chief
executive officer of Marion Laboratories, a major manufac-
turer of pharmaceutical, hospital, and laboratory products.
Since its founding some thirty years ago, its shareholders
have enjoyed a marvelous gain as sales and profits have
soared. Marion Laboratories began with just Ewing Kauffman but now employs nearly two thousand. In 1984 it was
listed in the book *100 Best Companies to Work for in America.*

Ewing Kauffman started his career as a salesman. He was
so successful that by the end of his second year his

commissions were higher than the president's salary. So the president reacted by reducing commissions. This turned out to be a switching point in Kauffman's life. He might have submitted to the unfair treatment. Instead, he dared to strike out alone and start his own company. He built Marion Laboratories upon unusual but sound management and ethical principles. Its success is a stunning example of imagination and purpose—the classic tale of a farm boy who parlayed a policy of sharing with others into a personal fortune. Remembering his own experience, Kauffman has seen to it that those who produce for him share equitably in his profits. If they don't produce, however, they get out. But in the corporation's existence, there are now sixty-one millionaires among its employees.

Defining the magic in the Kauffman technique is not easy. As one company official put it, "Just listening to him, you have to believe in his ability to lead." Kauffman's intense commitment and disarming candor have produced an employee attitude which some observers describe as "close to hero worship."

Kauffman himself brushes off such comments. He insists he is "just a salesman," and adds, "but a darn good one." A few years back Phil A. Koury, a former newspaper reporter who interviewed him exhaustively, later remarked to an associate, "When Kauffman got through talking about his company, I almost offered to take off my coat and start counting pills. It wouldn't surprise me if Ewing Kauffman announced that he had discovered a new ocean. No one would believe him and on the following day he would produce it."

To Kauffman the uncommitted life, like Plato's unexamined life, is not worth living. He pushes management conventions aside when they appear to hobble his efforts or impede movement of his company. The thinking man captivates him: "You can't stop a man who thinks." He is not inclined to applaud his own successes; instead he credits the executives around him for company gains and progress.

The Golden Rule of treating others as you would want them to treat you is as old as the hills, and Kauffman applies it to everyone, not just to his associates. For years his company has bought a synthesized chemical in large quantities from the Eli Lilly Company. Eventually, Lilly built a plant to manufacture this chemical specifically for Marion. Then a surplus of the chemical began accumulating in Europe, and his purchasing people came to Kauffman suggesting that they buy from European sources at lower prices.

Kauffman asked them, "If you were Lilly, what would you want us to do?"

Their answer was, "Stick with us!"

"Then that's what we'll do," he said.

Within a year the surplus was gone and a shortage of the chemical developed for all those in the industry except Marion!

Making money for himself is a by-product of Kauffman's motivation. The medicines manufactured and distributed by his firm are the important thing to him. They save lives, reduce pain, and ease trauma. Employee morale is high. And much is given back to his city. Single-handedly, Kauffman has been financing Red Cross efforts in several communities to teach CPR, the technique for saving the lives of those in cardiac arrest.

For many years he has also poured money into the building of his baseball team, the Kansas City Royals.

To some, Kauffman's business theories have seemed a little pious.

"Well," he replies, "what's wrong with sharing with those

who helped you get where you are? There was a time when our company was small and did not appear very promising. It's not easy to get men to work for a company with that kind of outlook, and so they came on the speculation of the future. I told them that someday we would furnish them an automobile. Someday, we would have insurance, a profit-sharing plan, and someday they would buy stock. They agreed to risk their future with me, and that is a demonstration of faith no man can take lightly. They came on future expectations. We have lived up to our promises. By that, I mean a return is made for a person's dedication and trust. I have been criticized by a lot of my friends as being too lavish in the employee benefits we now provide. And it is true that those who apply themselves unswervingly to our task have been and are amply rewarded. But the answer is, which would you rather have, 50 percent of 90 million dollars or 100 percent of 2 million dollars? You share the success which you create."

Ewing Kauffman calls his corporation an uncommon company, which gives an insight into the thinking process of this sincere person who has dared to be different from the pack.

Those ambitious for success need to think long and hard about the type of person they want to be. Are you strong enough to be different? Will you be faithful to every trust? Is your commitment to integrity able to withstand the severest testing? The odds are greatly on the side of those who have fixed in their minds and emblazoned on their souls a positive answer to all such questions.

Look for a minute at the story of Adam and Eve. In the third chapter of Genesis, Adam was hiding from God because he had eaten the forbidden fruit. Now I'm confident that God knew where Adam was, yet he called out to him,

"Where are you?" But it was not an ordinary question—it was much more probing. God was asking Adam, "What kind of a person are you? Where are you coming from? Are you strong or weak, true or false?" God was investigating Adam's true character.

Adam, of course, showed himself to be spineless and unfaithful to God's trust. Here was a switching point in his life. Instead of concealment, he could have openly repented and asked for forgiveness. But he chose to hide and when he was discovered, he put the blame for his mistake upon his wife and even tried to blame God!

Adam replied to the Lord, "The woman whom thou gavest to be with me, she gave me fruit of the tree." That's the same as saying, "My wife is really at fault for what I did, Lord. And also, please remember that *you're* the one who gave me this woman in the first place."

Most of us are not unlucky enough to be tested as early in the game as was Adam. We have time now to think about the concepts expressed in the chapters of this book. Most of them do not require any major personality or character changes. It's more a matter of shifting priorities, recognizing that even a relatively small change now, in time can lead to an enormously different person. A shift of a few inches today, in the long run will produce a result that is many miles apart from what would otherwise have been.

We've talked a lot in the book about business success and the odds for it. There have been many stories related. Let me tell you one more story about the most successful man I ever knew.

He was born Joseph W. Gilbert, and everyone knew him as Joe. Joe went to work for his father-in-law, who owned several lunch-counter restaurants in Kansas City. Soon, however, ambitious for an establishment of his own, he acquired a downtown restaurant that was losing money. At that time it was surrounded by pawnbrokers, second-hand stores, and the like.

I don't know how early in life Joe decided that he would give unstintingly of his time and thoughts to others. But he was different from any other restaurateur in town. No food order, day or night, was prepared and served to a patron without passing Joe's personal scrutiny. And if not exactly right in every detail, back to the kitchen it went. Such integrity won him an increasingly loyal clientele.

In spite of such time-consuming attention to every customer, Joe still went out of his restaurant to talk to those working in the stores and shops around him. His friends multiplied, and soon his cafe became profitable.

He began to build his restaurant empire little by little, carefully selecting and training the personnel in each restaurant to make certain they would maintain his standard of personal care with each customer.

Success followed success. Before Gilbert died in 1983, his company, Gilbert-Robinson, Inc., owned over sixty restaurants, including such nationally known ones as Annie's Santa Fe, Houlihans's Old Place, Fedora's, and The Bristol. Today the company, owned by W. R. Grace & Company, continues to grow following the same good management principles.

Joe Gilbert was an easy person to be with. You might not have gauged him instantly as a remarkable man. You would just know after meeting him that you liked him. And then the chances were good that the next day a brief, handwritten note would arrive with some information that could be helpful.

He had friends from coast to coast, from corporation chairmen to cabbage growers. Nothing was too much trouble for him to help someone. Several years ago when I began speaking professionally, a friend of his, Tom Haggai, was to receive an award in St. Louis as the outstanding public speaker in the United States. Joe thought I should hear this gifted speaker. Joe was eighty years old then, but he insisted that we meet that morning at 6:30 A.M. to fly to St. Louis so he could personally introduce me. He wanted me to listen to and perhaps benefit from Haggai's great speaking skill.

Joe Gilbert truly enjoyed giving that kind of positive help to others. He derived immense satisfaction from it as it was a reflection of his own positive thinking. He was confident of his abilities, and he had that same faith in his friends. He was inspirational to all he met. That inspiration came from a deep religious conviction that God is love and will help those who turn to him.

All of this, when combined with Joe's lively sense of humor, was irresistible. He did not develop these qualities as he was becoming successful. It was the other way around. His success in business came about as a *result* of those characteristics.

I am certain that when Joe Gilbert stood before his maker for the final pronouncement, God must have stepped down from his tribunal and thrown his arms around Joe to welcome him into the highest of heavens.

Like Joe Gilbert, each of us will someday stand before that all-powerful judge. I tremble when I consider that I may hear the words: "My son, I gave you more at your birth than almost anyone who ever lived in any other century or in any other country. You were born free, in a land of great opportunity. You had loving parents, were raised and educated gently. You have been given luxuries to ease your life such as the world before you never knew. And I have had pass before you countless chances to love and to help others of my children. Now, tell me, my son, what did you do with that life that I loaned to you?"

Then after I have stammered through a pitiful recounting I will hear one of two pronouncements. God may very well say, "Depart from me, you wicked and slothful servant! Be cast into the outer darkness!" And that will be hell.

Or by some miracle, I may hear these blessed words, "Well done, good and faithful servant; you have been faithful over a little, I will set you over much; enter into the joy of your master." And in his presence, there will be heaven!

When we examine life and consider it in the long run, the odds for a successful conclusion are greatly on the side of those who believe in and follow the instructions of the Bible.